500

Simple Website

Hints, Tips, and Techniques

RotoVision

A RotoVision Book
Published and distributed by RotoVision SA
Route Suisse 9, CH-1295 Mies
Switzerland

RotoVision SA, Sales & Editorial Office
Sheridan House, 114 Western Road
Hove BN3 1DD, UK

Tel: +44 (0)1273 72 72 68
Fax: +44 (0)1273 72 72 69
E-mail: sales@rotovision.com
Web: www.rotovision.com

10 9 8 7 6 5 4 3 2 1

ISBN: 978-2-940378-32-6

Designed by Studio Ink
Art Director: Tony Seddon

Reprographics in Singapore by ProVision (Pte) Ltd.
Tel: +65 6334 7720
Fax: +65 6334 7721

Printed in Singapore by Star Standard Industries (Pte) Ltd.

500
Simple Website
Hints, Tips, and Techniques

The Easy, All-in-One Guide to those Inside
Secrets for Building Better Websites

Jamie Freeman

Contents

Introduction 6
Gallery One **8**
Gallery Two **10**

Web Design Basics

Starting out **12**
Web forums **18**
User testing your site **20**
The professional web design process **22**

Design

Beyond the visual **24**
Design inspiration **26**
Design copyright **39**

Production Techniques

Creating the site **44**
Aqua-style buttons **48**
HTML basics **50**
Caching **53**
PayPal and eBay **55**
Two-column layouts **56**
Three-column layouts **57**
Batch processing **58**
Hosting companies **62**
Code comments **63**
Custom bullet points **64**
Contact links **66**
Header and footer layout **68**
Lists **70**
Show your work online **72**

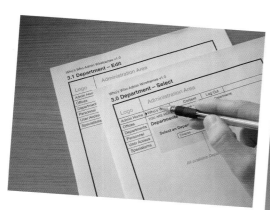

Accessibility and Web Standards

Inclusive web design **74**
Semantic markup **80**

Getting Found

Search engines **84**
Using Google **86**

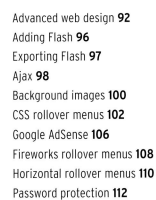

Cool Stuff

Advanced web design **92**
Adding Flash **96**
Exporting Flash **97**
Ajax **98**
Background images **100**
CSS rollover menus **102**
Google AdSense **106**
Fireworks rollover menus **108**
Horizontal rollover menus **110**
Password protection **112**
Image protection **115**
Hacking **116**
Flash portfolios **118**
PHP portfolios **120**

Featured designers 123
Glossary 124
Index 126
Acknowledgments 128

Introduction

500 Simple Website Hints, Tips, and Techniques concisely covers, in six parts, everything you need to know about website design.

When people hear the word "design" they often think only of visual design; what something looks like. However, visual design is just one part of the web design process. In fact, the visual design element of some projects usually only accounts for a small percentage of the work.

Not only is it just one small part of the process, but it tends to happen surprisingly late on. Consider a car designer who's been briefed to come up with a small family car. Even though they know some basics—it will have four wheels, five

seats, and an internal combustion engine—they still have a huge number of design considerations before they get to choose what color it will be!

It's the same with website design. You can probably make some basic assumptions—it will be accessed through some kind of web browser, users will click hyperlinks to navigate, etc.—but you have to design every aspect around the aims of the site and the users who will interact with it. In short, web design is not just how it looks but how it works too.

Of course, the lucky car designer occasionally gets asked to think outside the box and come up with a fabulous new concept vehicle. It might have six wheels, or none, fuel cell technology or solar power. Likewise, there might be occasions where you are tasked with designing a ground-breaking online experience which can throw all existing preconceptions to the wind. Good luck with that! Those projects are great fun, but are usually appropriate only

for very small target audiences. There is something of a trickle-down effect though, and yesterday's way-out techniques can become tomorrow's web standards.

Many of the hints, tips, and techniques in this book have taken me many years to learn. When I first started designing websites back in 1995 we were making it all up as we went along. That's still true to some extent today, but we now have the experience of all the people who went before us—their failures as well as their successes—to draw upon.

Of course, I'm still learning. This book won't tell you everything you need to know, but it will hopefully provide some inspiration along with valuable hints, tips, and techniques to get you well on the way to becoming a great website designer. Good luck, and in the language of the internet, :-)

P A T H O S

Written and directed by Dennis Cabella, Marcello Ercole, Fabio Prati
Produced and realized by Illusion

Watch the teaser: Small | Medium | Large

 Illusion

0000373

ARTIVA DES

GALLERY ONE

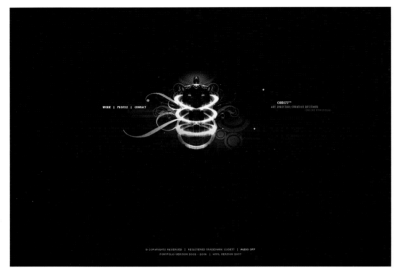

GALLERY TWO

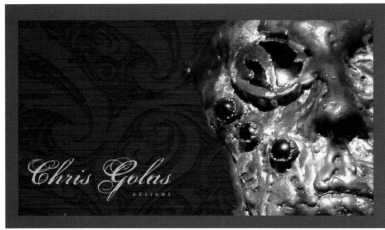

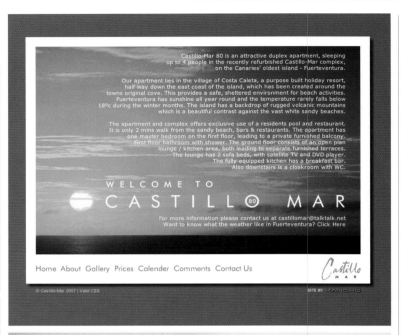

Web Design Basics

Starting out
This chapter will take you through some of the fundamentals of website design. It can be tempting to start building your site straight away, but trust me; this stuff is without question the most important aspect of creating a successful website. If you bear the following hints, tips, and techniques in mind throughout your project you are far more likely to come up with a great website, and far less likely to have to rebuild it a year down the line.

001 Planning

On big projects the planning phase can account for 60 percent of the time required for the whole job. But it's time well spent, and even if your project isn't particularly complicated, you should still take time to plan carefully from the start. It can save you a lot of headaches later on!

002 It's not a book!

Many designers coming from a print design background make the mistake of treating a website like it's a book, with one page logically following on from another. Remember that browsing websites is nonlinear; people jump from page to page, even from site to site, so all your pages need to be clear no matter what order they're viewed in.

003 Do you need a website?

Ask yourself if you really need a website. It may sound like an obvious question, but often people end up with sites simply because they feel they ought to have one; everyone else has got one, I want one too! In those cases the sites tend to wither on the vine as they are seldom updated and the content that is there can seem a little pointless.

004 What is your site for?

Before you start building your website, ask yourself this: what is it actually for? Whatever the answer, you will have a measure by which to judge whether the site is a success, and having that answer helps keep you on track during your project.

005 What is a home page?

A "home page" is the first page visitors usually see on a website, although people sometimes refer to their whole site as their home page, which confuses the issue. Be specific, and use the term correctly; it will help you communicate with other people involved with the project.

008 A taxonomy for your content

Taxonomy is the classification of organisms, relating them to one another in a logical system. For example, ants and beetles are both members of the insect family. Your content—especially if you have lots of it—needs to be similarly organized. For example, spanners and hammers are both tools, so you might choose to put them together in a section called "Tools." You could further classify them as handtools, to differentiate them from powertools, and so on.

006 Not everyone sees your home page

You can never be sure that people will see your home page first—if at all. They may have followed a link from another site that bypasses your home page; that's the beauty of the web! But bear this fact in mind when planning and designing your site, and provide clear navigation back to the home page.

007 Organizing your content

Don't be tempted to put every page in your main menu; too many choices will give your users information overload. Instead, you need to design a hierarchy, placing items within sections. This relieves the pressure on the menu, which now only needs to contain links to the sections.

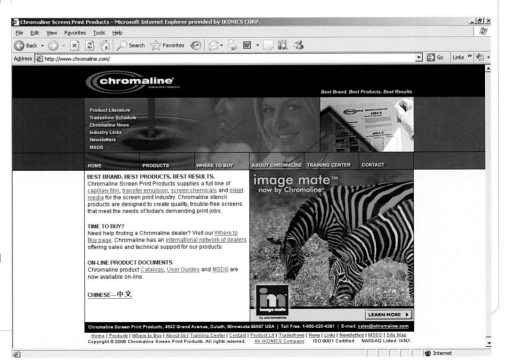

009 Dip a toe in the water

It's a good idea to dip a toe in the water before diving in. A good way to do this with web design is to try one of the free blogging services. You will get an idea of what it's like to put a site together, update it, style it, and so on. If you keep it up—and become frustrated with the restrictions these free services impose—then it's time to move into building "proper" websites.

010 Direct links from your home page

Once you've figured out a good hierarchy for your contents you might well have content deep in your site that needs to be more prominent. Don't be tempted to move that content into the main menu. Instead, create links on the home page—perhaps in the text, or even using graphic "flashes"—to draw attention to it, while maintaining the integrity of your "information architecture."

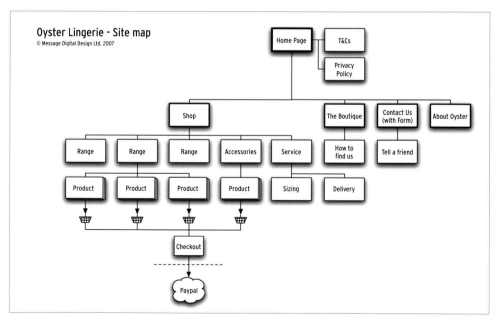

Oyster Lingerie - Site map
© Message Digital Design Ltd. 2007

011 Draw a site map

A site map is a great way to plan the overall structure of your site. It helps you group related items together to make it easier for your visitors to find their way around your site. A site map is also useful for showing to a client to help them visualize what you have in mind.

012 Don't try to fit everything in your site map

When you're designing your site, and perhaps creating a site map to show your client, don't be tempted to try and fit all the concepts of the site on one sheet of paper! If an area of your site is complex (perhaps a shopping process) then split off into another page, or consider full-blown wireframes (see tip 020).

013 Get help with the writing

If writing isn't exactly your strong point, ask a friend for help with bringing the copy up to standard. Remember, on the vast majority of websites the text is really what users visit for.

Katie Price Site Map

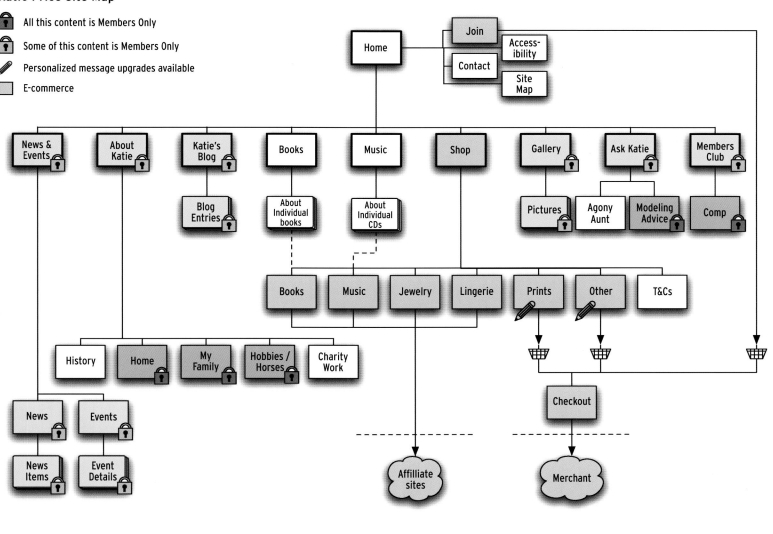

014 Identify your target audience

Before starting a new website, always ask yourself: who is this site aimed at? Once you have a clear idea of the intended audience you'll be able to plan accordingly. Without answering this question, your site may never quite hit the mark.

015 Site or page; what's the difference?

People often refer to "my web page" when what they usually mean is "my website." A website is made up of multiple pages that are linked together.

016 What's a menu for?

The purpose of the menu is to show people what's available in the site. It doesn't have to show every last thing on the site, but it must clearly show the types of thing that are available.

017 What's a submenu?

While the main menu shows what the site offers, the submenu shows the contents of a section within the site. For example, in a section called "Products" you would expect to see a submenu that listed those products.

018 Appropriate navigation

A site with thousands of pages needs sophisticated information architecture and navigation to allow users to find what they're after. But searches, cookie trails, subsections, submenus, and so on might all be overkill for a small site, so apply navigation techniques appropriate to the project.

019 Information architecture

Information architecture is the process of planning out where everything will go on your site, and how your users will navigate around it. Write down all the subjects your site will contain on post-it notes, then arrange them into groups that logically fit together.

020 Wireframes: the storyboards of web design

Filmmakers use storyboards to help plan out a movie. This process helps to ensure that what they're doing will work before they actually start filming. Wireframes are very similar to storyboards; they are simple outlines and boxes, often drawn by hand, laying out the main functions (e.g. navigation, search boxes, forms, etc.) of a site before you start to build it.

3.01 Section Index Page - example 2

LOGO		Contact | Media
		Help desk: 0123456789

YOU ARE HERE: Home > Housing & benefits

About the Council
Business Services
Community Services
Council Tax
▸ Housing & Benefits
Jobs
Leisure & Tourism
News
Parking & Transport
Planning
Recycling & Waste
Your Home & Environment

A-Z of Services
A B C D E F G H I J K L M
N O P Q R S T U V W X Y Z

Search
Enter text

Housing & Benefits
Lorem ipsum dolor sit amet

Lorem ipsum dolor sit amet consectuer adpiscing loreat. Lorem ipsum dolor sit amet consectuer adpiscing loreat. Dolor sit amet consectuer.

Apply for Housing Benefits
Frequently Asked Questions
Benefit Calculator

In this section:
Housing and council tax benefit
Council housing
Housing assistance

Housing and council tax benefit
Services
Lorem ipsum dolor sit amet
Consectuer adpiscing loreat
Adispum sit lorem

Information
Lorem ipsum dolor sit amet
Consectuer adpiscing loreat
Adispum sit lorem

Council housing
Services
Lorem ipsum dolor sit amet
Consectuer adpiscing loreat
Adispum sit lorem

Information
Lorem ipsum dolor sit amet
Consectuer adpiscing loreat
Adispum sit lorem

Housing assistance
Services
Lorem ipsum dolor sit amet
Consectuer adpiscing loreat
Adispum sit lorem

Information
Lorem ipsum dolor sit amet
Consectuer adpiscing loreat
Adispum sit lorem

Footer

021 Don't steal other people's content

Don't steal content from other people's websites. The copyright on everything you see on the web belongs to someone–photographs, illustrations, animations–and unless they give you permission to use it, you could be violating your local copyright laws.

022 Ask for permission

People can be surprisingly generous, and this is often especially true on the web. If you want to use an image you found on someone's website, just email them and ask if it's OK to do so. Offer them a credit with a link to their site and they'll probably be happy to oblige.

023 Don't be afraid to ask

If you see something cool on the web and wonder how it was done, why not ask the website designers responsible? Many designers will be happy to share their expertise; after all, experienced web designers were once beginners too.

Web Forums

024 Using forums

Forums on web design are a great place to pick up helpful information. You will often find plenty of people who have already been through the problems you might be facing and they'll be happy to help. One day, you might be the one passing on advice.

025 Choose the right forum

Busy forums often have different areas for different topics. For example, a web design forum may have specific areas on JavaScript, Usability, PHP Scripting, HTML, etc. Get to know the forum before you start posting to make sure you are in the right area.

026 Helping out on forums

As well as asking questions on forums, don't forget to answer them too. If you know the answer to someone's question then let them know; it's this "give and take" that makes forums work.

027 Mailing lists

Mailing lists are an alternative to forums. Instead of visiting a website to take part, emails are sent direct to your inbox. Some people prefer this as you get notified as soon as a new posting arrives. Also, the "threads" are always available on your computer even when you're not online.

028 Off-topic posting

Mailing lists are great for making friends too, but if you are discussing a subject that is not on the general topic of the list, preface your email subject line with "[OT]" to help busy people distinguish between important posts and chitchat.

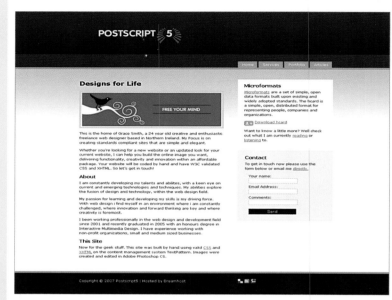

029 Using free website building services

For many people, using one of the free do-it-yourself website or blogging services is a great way to get online. A quick web search will show you which services are available.

030 Study others' source code

Every single programmer I've ever met learned their skills the same way: by studying the source code in other people's sites! Select "View Source" in your web browser and you can see the HTML, CSS, and even JavaScripts that have been used. Studying them is a great way to learn.

031 How much software do you need?

As a practical minimum you'll need three types of software: one for creating graphics, one for building the HTML pages, and one for uploading it all to your web server. Some packages combine two or more of these functions.

032 Find cheaper software alternatives

Professional software packages can cost huge amounts of money, but most of the work can be done with free or shareware alternatives. For example, I do all my handwritten code using BBEdit. This is available as a free version which includes most of the pro features.

033 Universal broadband?

Despite what the adverts imply, not everyone has broadband! It can be tempting to fill your site with 16Mb animations, but spare a thought for the majority of users who still get online using dial-up—especially true for rural, older, or poorer users.

034 Don't use visitor counters

We all want to know how many people visit our websites, but for the majority of us the answer is "not many!" So don't use a counter on your pages, use a web stats package instead. It will give you more information, look more professional, and save you potential embarrassment.

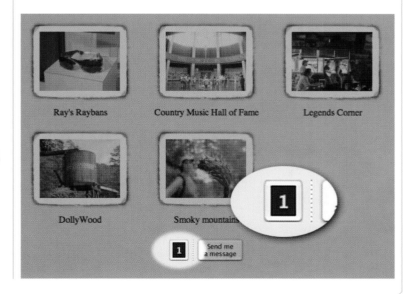

User testing your site

035 User testing

User testing (also called "usability testing") is carried out to ensure that your website will be usable by people in the real world. It's better to spot problems and fix them early on, preferably before your site is launched!

036 Jakob Nielsen

Jakob Nielsen is one of the leading experts on usability and his website is worth a look. It may not be the prettiest site in the world but he knows what he's talking about. You might not agree with everything he says (I know I don't!) but his "Top Ten Mistakes in Web Design" page makes for stimulating reading: www.useit.com/alertbox/9605.html

037 Basic user testing

A simple user test involves getting a few friends to try out your site before you launch it. Set them some tasks, such as "find a product and add it to your shopping cart," without prompting them as to how your site works. Make a note of any difficulties they encounter—and fix them!

038 Advanced user testing: 1

If your site is a professional project it's a good idea to carry out more thorough user testing to protect your client's investment. You should get between four and six test subjects of different ages and experience and set them all the same tasks to carry out on the site.

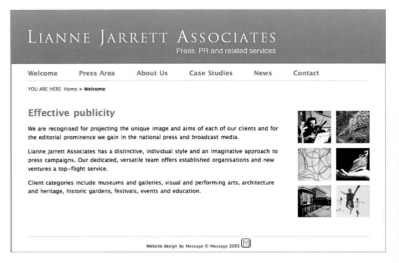

039 Advanced user testing: 2

Ideally, you should carry out at least two rounds of tests; one at the planning stage using paper mock-ups, and a second at the visual design stage before building the site. Implement any changes before moving on to the next stage, and use different people for each round of tests. A third round–carried out once the site is built, but before it is launched–should simply confirm what you have already found.

040 Video your user tests

Set up a video camera to record your user tests, pointing it at the screen. This will allow you to review your users' actions and judge the tests more objectively. It will also pick up their comments, which can be extremely instructive.

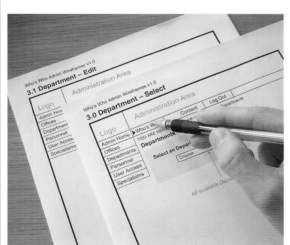

041 The house-building analogy

You can only add a certain amount onto an existing house before the original design scheme starts to break down. In extreme cases, even the very foundations might fail. At some point you have to tear it down and start again, designing the house you want from the ground up. The same holds true with web design.

042 When to use lists

If you find yourself writing out a series of related items, ask yourself if they represent a "list." If so, you should code them up correctly as an HTML list. A good example of a list is actually a menu; it is after all a list of pages in a website.

043 When to use ordered lists

If your list items also have a certain order (in other words, one naturally follows from another) you should consider using an ordered list. This will put numbers in front of the items, rather than just bullet points.

044 When to use tables

The simple answer is that you should use tables to present tabular data. Try to avoid using them if your information is just a simple list... use an HTML list instead! And under no circumstances should you use them simply for layout purposes.

The professional web design process

There are important steps to follow in order to see any web project through from concept to launch. You may not require all of them for smaller projects, but don't be tempted to skip steps that do apply–you'll only end up having to come back to do them anyway! The following tips are a rundown of all the tasks in a typical professional web design project.

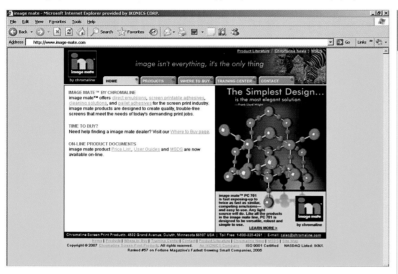

045 Step 1: a decent proposal

We usually start by responding to a client's request for a proposal. We take their brief, ask lots of questions, then write up an account of how we will approach the project. If they like our approach–and our price–we'll get the job and move on to the next step.

046 Step 2: planning

Once we've been awarded the job, we get down to some serious planning. This is mostly of a technical nature, deciding how we'll actually build the site. Will we use Flash? Do we need a database? How about a content management system? Does the client already have a web host? The answers to these questions help us to carry out the next step...

047 Step 3: project specification

This is quite simply the document that defines every aspect of the project. It's a working document which all parties refer to during the life of the project.

048 Step 4: wireframes

Now you know what the site needs to achieve (as laid out in the project specification) you can decide how it's going to achieve it, and illustrate this using the wireframes. For example, they will show the exact text that will appear on a button, or describe what a pop-up warning box will say.

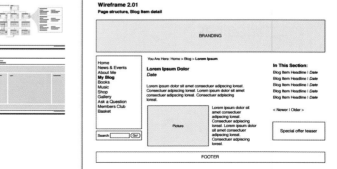

049 Step 5: usability testing

The wireframes are approved by the client, but before we spend all that time (and the client's money) building the site, hadn't we better test it? This is the perfect time to do a round of testing, using the wireframes as "paper prototypes."

050 Step 6: visual design

If you thought web design was all about creating graphics, you might be wondering why we're halfway through the project and have only just started to work out what the site will look like. If you didn't do all that preparation, it would be like deciding what a car will look like before you've thought about how many wheels it needs!

051 Step 7: site templates

Once the visual design is approved we will then make the CSS and (X)HTML templates that will control the look and feel of the finished site. These will be thoroughly tested for web standards-compliance and accessibility.

052 Step 8: more usability testing

The wireframes were tested and approved earlier in the project. So now we check that the visual design we have applied to them isn't going to compromise the usability of the system, for example, will users understand that funky flashing button? If not, now is the time to find out.

053 Step 9: site build

Incredible... we're up to step nine before we actually start building the website! This is where we make the HTML pages—or perhaps a database and content management system—that visitors will actually see. They won't see it quite yet though; there are some more steps to go through...

054 Step 10: acceptance testing

Once we've tested the site internally, we'll give our client access to it so that they can ensure it does everything they wanted. This is called "acceptance testing," and we normally ask them to sign a form stating that the site is all working correctly.

055 Step 11: launch

Often this is simply a case of uploading the files to a server, but it can be more complicated. For example, you may need to organize a domain name, or deal with an existing site. Plan ahead for this stage as it's too easy to get caught out right at the last hurdle.

Design

Beyond the visual

When some people hear the word "design" they think only of the visual aspect. Web design does of course involve a strong visual side, but it also requires design of the interaction between the site and the user.

This section addresses not just what a site looks like, but how it behaves, how it is organized, and a whole lot more.

056 Start with a design and stick with it

Don't start building your website until you've properly designed it. Otherwise you'll be tempted to take shortcuts that make your life easier, but don't necessarily make the website better.

057 The 10-second rule

You need to capture your visitors' attention—or give them what they're looking for—within 10 seconds of them arriving at your page. That's how long they're likely to afford you before heading back to the search engine they came from to try one of the countless other sites vying for their attention.

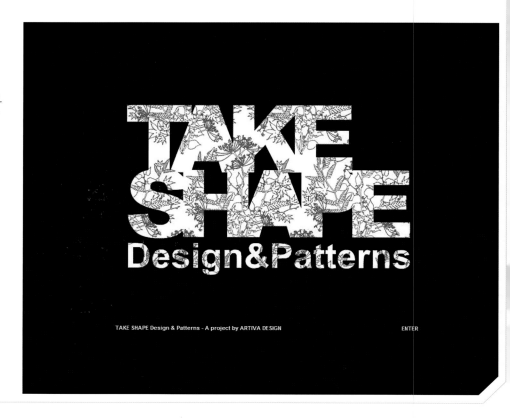

058 Avoid "rotating logo" syndrome

Software packages make it easy to create amazing-looking animations, but that doesn't mean they're a good idea. The thing that really marks an amateur website out from a professional one is that the former tend to use as many clever techniques as possible. It's very tempting to try out all these things when you're building your own website, but you don't have to try them all out on the same page!

059 Good photography can make the difference

Many otherwise good sites are let down by poor quality photography. If you can't get hold of decent photographs for your site, consider using one of the many royalty-free photo websites. Some are surprisingly cheap—or even free for use in personal projects.

060 Set the tone

Before you start designing, think about the feel you want your site to have. Write down the key words that describe what your site will look like: clean, professional, funky, lively, serious. Then refer to this list during the design process to make sure you're staying on track.

Design inspiration

061 All your sites needn't be the same

If you design a lot of websites, it can be easy to get stuck in a rut. Remember to treat each project individually; that way you'll end up with the site you need, rather than a site just like all your others.

062 Books can be a great source of ideas

The obvious place to look for inspiration for great web design is online, but there are plenty of excellent books showcasing good web design too. The writers have gone to the trouble of scouring the best—and the worst!—of the web, so you don't have to.

063 Use a digital camera for inspiration

If you're feeling lost for inspiration, try snapping a few digital images as a starting point. Take them into Photoshop and start trying out those effects! An extreme close-up of a flower, a blurry picture of a child's toy, clouds, fabric, leaves... the possibilities are endless, and you can end up with a unique image to incorporate into your design.

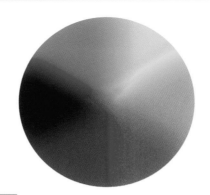

064 Complementary colors

A basic understanding of color theory can help even the most experienced designer. Complementary colors—those which you can be sure will work well with each other—lie opposite each other on a standard color wheel. You can use these as a jumping-off point when working on a new design.

065 Beyond web safe colors

The vast majority of computer systems can now display many thousands of colors, so the limited "web safe" color palette is no longer really required. Even the designer who first identified the web safe color schemes has now abandoned them (see www.lynda.com/hex.asp).

066 Round corners for a softer feel

Rounding off the corners of panels on the page can make an otherwise harsh design more approachable, especially if combined with friendly, bright colors.

067 GIF image compression

GIF image compression works best when there are large areas of the same color in the image. It does this by treating adjacent identical pixels as a group, rather than individual pixels, resulting in a smaller file.

068 Fewer colors mean smaller GIFs

Reduce the size of GIF images by limiting the number of colors used. Not all images need the full GIF range of 256 colors, so experiment with reducing the number until the image starts to suffer. Try selecting 128, 64, or even as few as four colors. You'll be amazed how few colors you can get away with.

069 Making smaller JPEG files

JPEG compression works by "blurring" areas of low detail in an image—such as a blue sky—to reduce the amount of data needed. You can help this process by subtly blurring the less important areas of your images before setting the JPEG compression level.

070 Selective JPEG compression

Some image-editing software can perform "selective" JPEG compression. This means you can set certain areas of the image at higher or lower compression levels, depending on how important that area of the image is. For example, a face could be left at a higher quality, while the background was more compressed.

071 Resizing images on the page

Although you can resize an image using HTML (by editing the width and height attributes) it generally creates ugly, pixellated results. It's much better to resize your image using an image editor such as Fireworks, Photoshop, Image Ready, etc., first.

072 Balance image quality with file size

Make sure your image files are no larger than they need to be. You might decide that your main product photo needs to be high quality and so is worth the extra download time. But if it's too big, people might not wait to download it.

073 Navigation conventions can be helpful

Imagine if you bought a car and couldn't find the door handle—that's what some websites can feel like. Using navigation conventions might seem like a design cop-out, but your users will thank you for it.

074 Reuse images

If you have the same graphic appearing in lots of places on your site, you don't need a separate GIF or JPEG for each one. Simply refer to the same image each time.

075 Reusing images power tip

You can take image reuse one stage farther when working on your visual design. If your concept has several slightly different graphics, could you standardize them without harming the look of your site? If so, great; you've saved yourself some work, and saved your users some download time.

076 Reusing transparent GIFs

GIF images have the ability to include transparent areas. This means you can reuse a single image on different colored backgrounds to create more variation while also reducing download size.

077 Replace an existing image

If you want to replace an image on your website, you can sometimes do it without having to edit your page. Simply create an image of the same dimensions and upload it to your web space. If you name the new image exactly the same as the original it will simply replace it, so next time you look at the page the new image will appear. Remember: if the content or meaning of the image has changed you may need to edit the alt text in the page HTML.

078 Replacing text with images

If you really need to preserve the look of a special font that is not commonly installed in web browsers you can use a GIF or JPEG image instead. But remember to include alt text that is identical to that displayed in the image.

079 Alternative sans-serif font

My personal favorite sans-serif font is Lucida. It's a little different to the standard Arial, and looks much more pleasing than Verdana at larger sizes.

Lucida Grande
The quick brown fox jumps over the lazy dog

Arial
The quick brown fox jumps over the lazy dog

Verdana
The quick brown fox jumps over the lazy dog

080 Alternative serif font

I often use Georgia as an alternative serif font in place of the more classic Times. It has a slightly more modern feel and is very widely installed, so most users will be able to see your site as intended.

Georgia
The quick brown fox jumps over the lazy dog

Times
The quick brown fox jumps over the lazy dog

081 Ultra-thin keylines

To make a keyline appear thinner than one pixel, try using a lower percentage of the color. For example, rather than a white line on a black background, try the line in a shade of gray instead.

| 100% White |
| 75% White |
| 50% White |
| 25% White |

082 Use Verdana at small font sizes

Verdana is great to use for small font sizes. I use it for things like "breadcrumb trails" or additional navigation in the page footer, but it starts to look a bit clunky for body text at about 12px.

083 Using GIFs for text

If you need to create a graphic to replace some text–for example, if you need to use a font that's not "web safe"–then the GIF format is virtually always the best image format to use. It will generally create smaller, crisper files for this kind of graphic image.

084 Web safe fonts

Certain fonts are available as standard across most computer operating systems but the range of truly web safe fonts is very limited. Whichever font you choose, ensure that substitute fonts are included in your list.

085 Web safe colors

Web safe colors are a limited range of hexadecimal colors designed to display consistently across older 8-bit color computer systems. To be absolutely certain your design will display correctly even on older machines you should think about using them; this could be a consideration if your target audience is in the developing world, for example.

086 When to use the GIF image format

GIF images use a limited color range (a maximum of 256 colors) so are best suited to graphic images such as logos and background patterns, rather than photographs. Also, GIF images can be animated–unlike JPEGs.

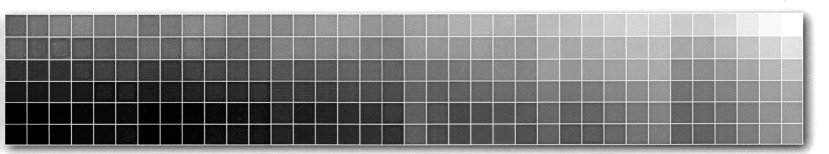

087 When to use JPEG images

The JPEG image format is especially suited to pictures with a very wide range of colors. For example, photographs with lots of natural shading will usually render much more realistically in JPEG rather than GIF format.

088 Work it out with a pencil

Don't let your design be led by what your software can do. Start out by using paper and a pencil. It might seem old-fashioned, but it means you get the idea straight from your head, not filtered through restrictions that the software imposes on you.

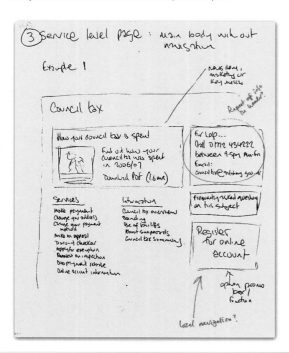

089 Limit your color palette

If your design uses lots of colors it is likely to be too busy-looking and difficult on the eye. Limit your palette to two or three main colors, plus black and white, to achieve a more professional look.

090 Expand your color palette!

Create a fun, busy design by using a rainbow of different colors. Done well, your design could look like a bowl of candies, creating an attractive, jolly atmosphere. (Done badly, it could look a real mess, so pick your colors carefully.)

* AD.PROJECT

AD.PROJECT*
Self published promotionals...

Cataloghi/Brochure/Cartoline:
DO YOU UNDERSTAND?
(W)3=?
CATCH'EM ALL
AD.B.06
GRAPHIC LOOPS & CUT UPS
AD.B.05
SPIRALBOOK
INDUSTRIAL ARCHEOLOGY

CD-Rom:
AD.05
AD.04

Animation:
BALCKBUNNY
BRUM BRUM

Pin:
MONKEY
MONKEYPANTHER
TREE

Digital Experiment:
BUBBLE GUM

ARTIVA DESIGN
AD.PROJECT
PORTFOLIO
PREVENTIVI
PUBBLICAZIONI
PC GOODIES

*Selezione

094 Color tints for a consistent palette

Rather than use lots of different colors, use tints of your main colors to help maintain a consistent feel to your design. For example, if your main color is a nice strong green, you could use a 25 percent tint of that color to create panels.

095 How opacity works

If you have a color block that is a 20 percent tint of your main color and you overlay it on another similar tint block, the area of overlap will now be a 40 percent tint of the main color. You can use this method to build up interesting shapes, tints, and graduations.

091 Don't rely on color alone

If you choose to color code your sections, make sure that users with visual impairments (e.g. blindness or color blindness) can still differentiate the sections clearly. Don't rely on color alone; use clear text headings as well.

092 Color-coded sections

Help users differentiate between sections in your site by color coding them. For example, a color bar across the top of the pages could change, depending on which section you are in.

093 Avoid pale colors for text

If you have created a color-coded menu, make sure all the colors are deep enough to be read easily. Maintain a good level of contrast between the text and the background color.

Drop shadows

096 Add a drop shadow to an image

The easiest way to give your images a soft drop shadow is to add one in your image-editing software (e.g. Photoshop). Resize the canvas to add room around the image. Create a new layer, use the marquee tool to make a rectangle the same size as the image, and fill it with mid-gray. Blur the layer to soften the edges of the rectangle, and move it behind the original image layer. Offset it to the bottom right, and you're done.

097 Consistent drop shadows

If all the images in your site are going to have the same drop shadow effect, it makes sense to keep the effect consistent; the same shade of gray, the same amount of blur, and so on. This kind of attention to detail is what makes a really good design stand out.

098 Make a drop shadow template

Once you've worked out the style of shadows you want all your pictures to have, create a template in your image-editing software. This file will have a shadow all ready to go; all you need to do is drop your image in. Create both portrait and landscape versions so that you can handle most types of image without having to go back to basics.

099 Create custom table styles

If your site is going to have tables showing facts and figures it's worth spending some time working out a design for them that fits in with the overall look and feel of the rest of the site. Overriding the default table styles can make a real difference to the overall "design" quality of your project.

Item	Description	Price
Widget	Stainless steel, flanged, gloss	6.99
Grommet	Aluminum, tapered	17.99
Socket	Flame retardant, inflatable	7.49
Pocket	Standard fit, pack of 6	0.99 (each)
Wicket	Adjustable, reversible	1.29

Item	Description	Price
Widget	Stainless steel, flanged, gloss	6.99
Grommet	Aluminum, tapered	17.99
Socket	Flame retardant, inflatable	7.49
Pocket	Standard fit, pack of 6	0.99 (each)
Wicket	Adjustable, reversible	1.29

Item	Description	Price
Widget	Stainless steel, flanged, gloss	6.99
Grommet	Aluminum, tapered	17.99
Socket	Flame retardant, inflatable	7.49
Pocket	Standard fit, pack of 6	0.99 (each)
Wicket	Adjustable, reversible	1.29

100 Creating a "page" look

Create a centered "page" with drop shadows. First make an image 1,024 pixels wide and 10 pixels high. Fill it with gray, and create a central white area 800 pixels wide. Place a blend from black to gray on either side of the white area. Use this image as the background in your CSS, repeating vertically.

101 A page look that expands

Rather than a white page area that extends the full height of the browser window, you can make one that expands. The technique is similar except that you need to assign the background to a **<div>** rather than the page. The div will only extend down as far as the content requires.

102 Add a bottom shadow to expanding page design

Create a graphic similar to before but 20 pixels high. Make a white block 10 pixels high and 800 pixels wide at the top of the image, and add the black-to-gray fade on all sides. Make an empty **<div>** called **#footer** and assign the new image as the background. Place this after the div containing the page background and the two should match up, creating a seamless drop shadow around the bottom and sides.

103 Creating the top of the page design

Follow the same technique used for creating the page bottom to add a top to your design. You can duplicate the footer image and rotate it 180 degrees rather than start from scratch.

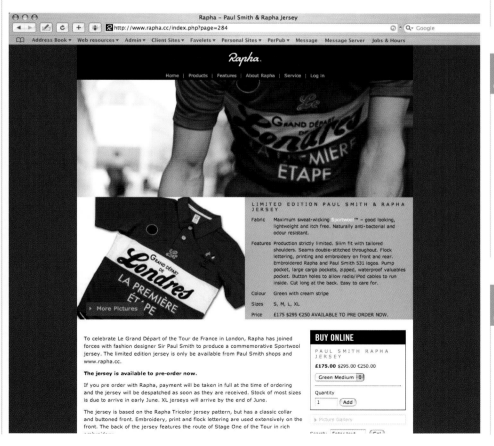

104 Fixed width design

Websites that have a pre-set width are known as "fixed width" designs. These do not expand or contract with the size of the browser window, which means the designer has more control over things like column widths. A drawback is that the space either side of the content can look bare and uninspiring. It also denies users the option to resize the site to their own preferences.

105 Liquid design

So-called "liquid" designs expand to fill the available window space. This puts a certain amount of control in the hands of the user; if they want the full-screen experience for your site they can have it. A common drawback with this type of design is that column widths can become very wide, making them hard to read.

106 Combining liquid and fixed designs

A combination of fixed and expanding columns can result in a hybrid liquid and fixed width design. For example, you could fix the width of the left-hand menu, while allowing the main content area to expand.

107 Limit the expansion in liquid designs

Consider setting a maximum width to limit the extent to which your layout will expand. This can stop a column width getting out of hand on some of the extremely wide monitors now available.

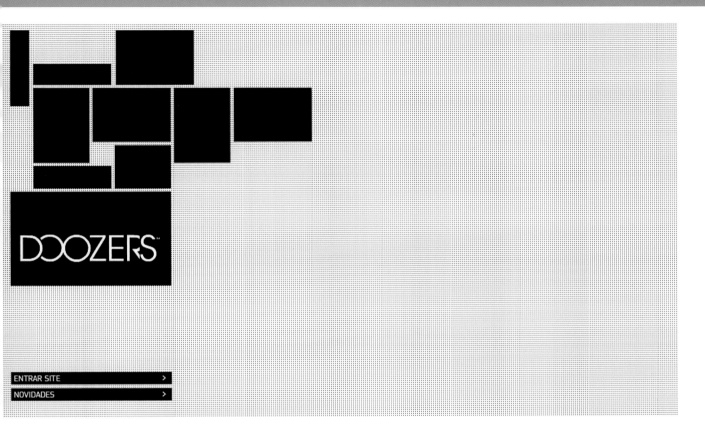

108 Implementing maximum width

Set the maximum width of a **\<div\>** by typing this into your CSS:

#myColumn { max-width: 800px; }

Now assign the id "myColumn" to the **\<div\>** around your content and it won't stretch beyond 800 pixels wide, no matter how wide the user's browser window is. However, it will still contract if their window is smaller than that.

109 Consistent image sizes

Rather than having images in all shapes and sizes, set consistent dimensions to help the design feel cleaner and more organized. For example, all your images could be 320 x 240 pixels (landscape or portrait) while the thumbnail versions could be 80 x 60 pixels.

110 4 x 3 format images

Most digital cameras produce images in 4 x 3 format. The short edge of such images is 75 percent the length of the long edge. Here are some examples of 4 x 3 image sizes:
- 320 x 240 pixels
- 640 x 480 pixels
- 800 x 600 pixels

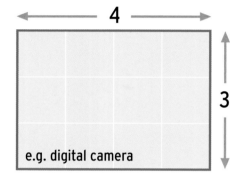

e.g. digital camera

111 SLR image formats

Digital SLR cameras produce images in slightly different formats to that of consumer digital cameras. Rather than 4 x 3 format, they use 3 x 2, or close variants thereof. Here are some examples of 3 x 2 image sizes:
- 300 x 200 pixels
- 540 x 360 pixels
- 720 x 480 pixels

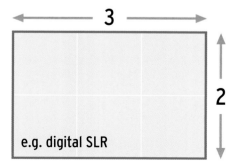

e.g. digital SLR

112 4 x 3 aspect ratio movies

Most video on the web is presented in 4 x 3 aspect ratio. As this is the same as most digital camera images, it's a good idea to standardize on this ratio for all images and movies on your site.

113 16 x 9 aspect ratio movies

Although most movies on the web (and TV) are shown in 4 x 3 aspect ratio, an increasing amount are being shown in 16 x 9 "widescreen" ratio. The ratio you choose will depend on the format the video was shot in; it's vital to use the same aspect ratio or the movie will appear either stretched or squashed.

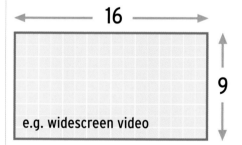

e.g. widescreen video

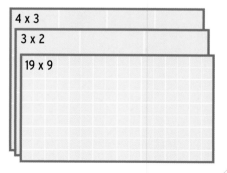

114 Link the logo to your home page

Users are getting used to the idea that clicking the website logo—when placed in the top left-hand corner—will take them back to the home page. Following this simple convention will help make your site that little bit more usable.

115 Include a "home" link too

As well as making your logo into a link to the home page, you should also include an explicit "home" link in the menu.

Design copyright

116 Protecting your copyright

Copyright automatically resides with the creator of an original work, whether it's a poem, a painting, or a website. You don't have to do anything to protect your copyright, but putting a notice on your work will make it clear to everyone that you are aware of your rights.

117 Be clear about copyright ownership

If you are designing a website for a paying client, they might assume they will own the copyright in the site, but unless stated otherwise the copyright actually remains with the designer. It's best to be clear about these issues up front to make sure there are no misunderstandings later down the line.

118 Assigning copyright

You can assign your copyright over to a client if they so wish, but this permanent transfer of ownership of your intellectual property (IP) should be reflected in the price you charge them.

119 Copyright notices

The footer is also a good place for putting a copyright notice. This could be something along the lines of "Website copyright Jamie Freeman © 2009."

120 Check the radius of rounded corners

Some software can distort the radius of rounded boxes, leading to ugly corners that aren't based on a simple quarter circle. To avoid this, recreate the box from scratch at the correct size, or make a normal box, then apply rounded corners to it.

Pleasing Radii

Distorted corners

Mmm... consistent

Eew... random!

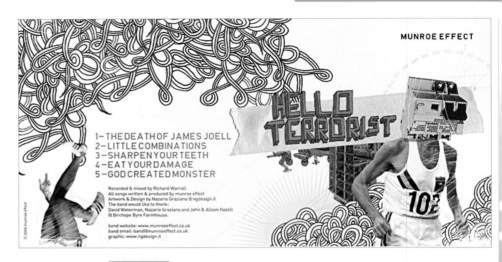

MUNROE EFFECT

1– THE DEATH OF JAMES JOELL
2– LITTLE COMBINATIONS
3– SHARPEN YOUR TEETH
4– EAT YOUR DAMAGE
5– GOD CREATED MONSTER

Recorded & mixed by Richard Worrall
All songs written & produced by munroe effect
Artwork & Design by Nazario Graziano @ ngdesign.it
The band would like to thank:
David Waterman, Nazario Graziano and John & Alison Hazell
@ Birchope Byre Farmhouse.

band website: www.munroeeffect.co.uk
band email: band@munroeeffect.co.uk
graphic: www.ngdesign.it

© 2006 munroe effect

121 Consistent round-cornered boxes

Try to stick to a limited set of radii when creating a design with round corners. This will help the design look more "considered" and professional, because an assortment of different corner styles can look messy and is difficult on the eye.

122 Custom submit buttons

Rather than have the default submit button that the operating system provides, you can use a graphic instead. This gives you more control over the the look and feel of the site, as the button can match your design more closely.

123 Drawbacks of custom submit buttons

Be aware that users are used to seeing standard Windows or Mac OS submit buttons, and they might not immediately understand what your custom-designed ones mean. You need to ensure that your custom-designed buttons are clear and meaningful.

124 Consider screen size

In the early days we would design all sites so that they would fit in a 640 x 480 pixel screen resolution. That soon crept up to 800 x 600, and now we tend to optimize for 1,024 x 768 (although most of our sites will happily work on an 800 pixel wide screen). 1,024 x 768 is by far the most popular screen resolution, but remember those on smaller screens and devices such as cellphones.

125 Remember scroll bars in screen size

If you are designing to a particular screen size (e.g. 1,024 x 768 pixels) remember to allow for a scroll bar. Your actual design should be at least 30 pixels narrower than the target screen size.

126 What is "rollover?"

"Rollover"—also known as "mouseover" or "hover"—is a visual effect that occurs when the user places their mouse over an active area of the screen, such as a link (**<a>** tag).

127 Rollover link styles

When designing the hover "state" for links you can change any aspect of the styling—color, size, weight, capitalization, and so on. However, these can lead to behaviors that cause problems for the user. For example, if your link text becomes bigger or bolder when you mouse over it, all of the text around it may have to move to make room for it, so it's probably best avoided.

128 Use custom bullet points

It's not particularly tricky to implement custom bullet points (see tips 237–240), but it's the kind of detail that often gets overlooked. The bullet points don't need to be flashy, they just need to match your overall design scheme.

129 Make it look like a button!

If you are designing a replacement for standard operating system submit buttons, don't stray too far from the usual styles. For example, a slight three-dimensional effect or shadow reminds users of the buttons they're used to seeing, and this helps your design to be more usable while still fitting in with the overall look and feel of the site.

130 Maximum width with percentages

As well as defining an absolute maximum width in pixels, you can set a relative width by using percentages. This offers a reasonable compromise between fixed and liquid designs. The CSS is very similar to before, but with a percentage value (%) replacing the pixel (px) value:

#myColumn { max-width: 75%; }

131 Mixing colors using opacity

If your design uses two main colors you can use transparent tint panels overlaid on one another to "mix" the two colors together. For example, a 50 percent blue panel laid over a 50 percent red panel will give you a purple panel. Assuming your main colors are "complementary" this new middle color should sit nicely in your color scheme.

132 Picking color tints

Most graphics programs allow you to set the opacity of an element. Create a panel in your main color, then reduce the opacity until it reaches the desired tint. Use the eyedropper to "sample" that color, then drop it into the elements you want in that tint using the paint bucket tool.

133 Repeating background patterns

Repeating background patterns can look clunky unless they're carefully designed as you generally don't want to see the repeat point. Rather than trying to base a pattern on part of a photo, you might find a geometric design easier to control, and subtler patterns with less contrast will often work better.

134 Nonrepeating background images

You can get away with having large, nonrepeating background images as long as you compress them fairly heavily to keep the file size down. Slightly blurred images work best for this, as it will make any overlaying text easier to read.

135 Room for expansion

Your site might be small today, but what does the future hold? If the plan is for the content to expand, perhaps even to include different types of content, then you should plan the site to allow for that from the start. Changing the structure of your site is much more risky to do once it's up and running.

136 Simple CSS drop shadows

Add the following to a style for adding drop shadows to all images:

img.dropShadow { background: url(images/dropShadow.gif) right bottom no-repeat; }

Add **class="dropShadow"** to the **<img>** tag for each image, and ensure that the image is slightly smaller than the dropShadow.gif image or it will not be able to peek out from behind.

137 Put credits in the footer

If you wish to credit yourself as the builder of your sites it's common practice to do this in the footer. Keep the text small and avoid large logos; you don't want to draw too much attention to it, but people who want to find out who built the site will know where to look.

138 Turn your credit into a link

As well as putting a credit line in the footer, turn your name into a link to your main website. This will not only make it easier for people to visit you, but it will also add to your search engine ranking to have the additional in-bound links.

139 Use square cropped images for thumbnails

If you have a gallery that uses thumbnail images, a mixture of landscape and portrait thumbnails can look really messy. A solution is to crop all the images to a suitable square (carefully preserving the important part of the image), enabling a much neater thumbnail layout.

140 Using drop shadows on images

Careful use of soft drop shadows on images can lift them from the page and give the design a really professional touch.

141 Using CSS for drop shadows

If all the images are the same size you can create a CSS style to automatically place a shadow behind each image in your site. Again, create styles for both portrait and landscape format images.

142 Code coloring

Although you can edit HTML in any plain text editor, most dedicated HTML editing software will display the code in different colors. This allows you to easily differentiate between a table, for example, and a link.

```
// Display the message on screen:

echo '<p>You have sent the following message to ';
echo $recipient;
echo ':<br /><em>';
echo stripslashes($_GET['sender_message']);
echo '</em></p>';
```

143 Custom code coloring

You can specify the colors your HTML editor uses for displaying tags in code view, creating a palette that suits your own preferences.

Production Techniques

Creating the site
Now that you've planned and designed your website project, it's time to start putting it all together. This section deals with the nuts and bolts of web design to help you actually create your site.

144 Read the manual

You're itching to get started using your new web software, but take some time to read the manual before leaping in. If you don't know what your software is capable of, how will you get the best out of it? At least read the "Quick Start Guide!"

145 Cascading Style Sheets (CSS)

Cascading Style Sheets are used to describe the way your web pages will look. Although you can include CSS within your HTML page, it's a much better idea to link your page to a separate CSS document.

146 Anatomy of an HTML page: 1

All elements within an HTML page are contained within tags; either a pair of opening and closing tags like this: **`<p>Hello world</p>`** or a single self-closing tag, like this:
`<img src="mypicture.jpg" >`

Above: a screenshot of SweetCMS in action

This site is itself built and maintained exclusively using sweetCMS. Take a look at SweetCMS features in action to see just how easy and powerful it is in use.

147 Anatomy of an HTML page: 2

An HTML page starts with a document declaration, telling the web browser what to expect. For example, a standards-compliant (X)HTML page would begin like this:

`<!DOCTYPE HTML PUBLIC "-// W3C//DTD HTML 4.01//EN" "http://www.w3.org/TR/1999/ REC-html401-19991224/strict. dtd">`

148 Anatomy of an HTML page: 3

All the content of the page would be contained within a pair of opening and closing tags, like this:

<html>Page content here...</html>

149 Anatomy of an HTML page: 4

The **<head>** tags are the first content to appear within the **<html>** tags, and these define the title of the page, followed by any "meta" information, such as keywords and page description:

<title>Jamie Freeman - My Home Page</title>
<meta name="Description" content="The home page of Jamie Freeman, featuring my music, weblog, photos, and favorite links. " />
<meta name="Keywords" content="music, acoustic guitar, songwriting, mod, scooters" />

Notice that the **<meta>** tags are self-closing.

150 Anatomy of an HTML page: 5

Still in the **<head>** tags, you might find a **<link>** tag, which links the page to an external Cascading Style Sheet (CSS) file:

<link href="layout.css" rel="stylesheet" type="text/css" />

151 Anatomy of an HTML page: 6

After all of that, we finally get to the content people will actually see on the page! This is all contained within the **<body>** tag, like so:

<body>Your page content here...</body>

152 Anatomy of an HTML page: 7

Within the body tag you'll find tags for headings, paragraphs, lists, images, links, and so on. Here are some sample tags:

<h1>...</h1> This is a main heading.
<p>...</p> This is a paragraph of text.
<a>...</a> This is an "anchor" (link).

153 Anatomy of an HTML page: 8

Once you get to the end of your HTML page you'll see the closing tags for a couple which were opened right at the start, namely the **<body>** and **<html>** tags, like this:

</body>
</html>

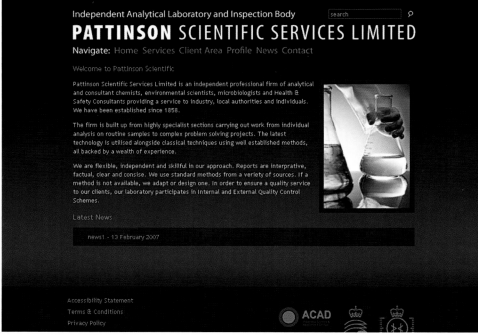

154 How to tell opening and closing tags apart

An opening tag looks like this: **\<h1>**. A closing tag is almost the same, but it has a slash added after the first angle bracket, like this: **\</h1>**.

155 Tags can have additional parameters

Add additional parameters to tags to associate a style with the specific instance of the tag. For example **\<p class="intro">**. If you had a style called intro it would be applied to all such tags, while regular **\<p>** tags would not be styled.

156 Where to use CSS "classes"

You use classes where you have a number of similarly styled elements on the same page. For example, you might want all images (**\<img>**) to have the same outline style. Or you might want to display all email links (**\<a>**) with a mail icon.

159 Animated GIFs can get big

Each frame in your animated GIF can add as much to the file size as a regular static GIF. So a 10-frame animation could be 10 times bigger than a regular GIF!

160 No spaces in CSS style names

The CSS specification doesn't allow spaces in style names, but names like **.emaillink** can be hard to read. There are several ways around this, including underscores (**.email_link**), hyphens (**.email-link**), and "camel case" (**.emailLink**). It's called camel case because of the "hump" created by the capital letters in the middle!

157 Where to use CSS "ids"

You use ids where you will only have a single instance of an element on the page. For example, you would only have one main navigation menu, so you could create a style for it—**<div id="menu">**. Other examples include footers, headers, breadcrumb trails, etc.

158 CSS "float"—what is it?

Assigning a "float" to a box (e.g. a **div**) has the effect of aligning it to the left or right of its container element (e.g. the page, another **div**). It's rather like the align property in an image tag.

Aqua-style buttons

161 Easy aqua-style buttons

Buttons that emulate the "aqua" style popularized by Apple's Mac OS can make a design look really professional. Here's an easy way to get the effect in just three steps.

162 Aqua-style buttons: step 1

Create a rectangle with completely round ends, filled with a strong color that fades from dark at the top, to slightly lighter at the bottom.

163 Aqua-style buttons: step 2

Add a second round-ended rectangle that fades from white at the top to transparent at the bottom. This should be slightly less wide than the original and about half as high. Place it near the top of the first rectangle.

164 Aqua-style buttons: step 3

Create a drop shadow on the first rectangle, but rather than the usual gray, this time make it the same color as the button itself. This will give the impression of light passing through a transparent object and being cast onto the page behind.

165 Image formats with transparency

Both GIF and PNG image formats support some level of transparency. With GIFs the transparency is quite crude, but the format is very widely supported. With PNG, the transparency is much more controllable, but older browsers do not support it.

166 GIF transparency

GIF transparency is "binary." In other words, the transparency is either on or off on certain parts of the image. It works well for simple shapes where the background color roughly matches the image, but you can't create subtle image-fading effects using GIFs. In these cases, PNG might be a better option.

167 PNG "alpha" transparency

PNG files support "alpha" transparency. This format has an extra color channel in addition to the usual red, green, and blue (RGB), known as the Alpha channel. This channel contains grayscale data where the shades of gray relate to the transparency (or opacity) of the image, allowing very subtle fading effects to be used.

168 When to use GIF transparency

GIF transparency is suitable for:
- Text headings
- Logos
- Hard-edged graphic devices
- Images where transparency is *vital*

The last point relates to the fact that virtually *all* web browsers support this file format.

169 When to use PNG transparency

PNG transparency is suitable for:
- Photographs with vignette effects
- Soft-edged graphic devices
- Images where transparency is a noncritical enhancement

The last point relates to the fact that some older web browsers do not support PNG transparency. (The really old ones don't support PNG *at all*.)

170 Transparency with animated GIFs

GIF images can also be animated, and the transparency can animate too. Each frame of the animation has its own transparency.

171 How animated GIFs optimize

There's a clever trick animated GIFs can perform, and that's the way in which identical areas from one frame to another can be shared in order to keep the file size down. Bear this in mind when designing your animation; if a large area of the GIF remains static it can keep the file size down. Conversely, if large areas change from frame to frame, the file size is likely to be much larger.

172 Optimizing animated GIFs

When you optimize an animated GIF, remember to check each frame. What looks good for the first frame might not necessarily look the best for subsequent frames. You may need to choose a different number of colors, or a different palette that works better across all the frames in the sequence.

HTML basics

173 WYSIWYG HTML editors

Most dedicated HTML editing software provides a "What You See Is What You Get"–or WYSIWYG (pronounced "whizzywig")–mode. Similar to using a word processor, it makes creating web pages much easier, allowing you to concentrate on content and layout while it creates the HTML code behind the scenes.

174 HTML editing

Learn some basic HTML; at some point you will need to know what's going on "under the hood" and it will give you a much better understanding of how your site works. It also helps you to fix problems when things go wrong.

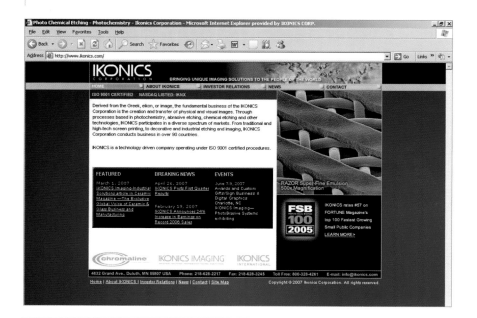

175 HTML basics: what is it?

HTML stands for hypertext markup language. It consists of simple "tags" surrounding your text, which describe the content of the document to the web browser.

176 HTML basics: tag types

There are two types of HTML tag. Some have two parts, like this:

`<opening tag>Page content</closing tag>`

This type usually surrounds visible text on a page. Notice that backslash in the closing tag? Others self-close, like this example, which puts a new line within a block of text: **`<br />`**

177 HTML basics: bold and italic text

To make some text stand out, you can make it strong (bold) or give it emphasis by making it italic. The following code shows how to achieve these effects:

`<strong>This makes your text bold</strong>`
`<em>This makes your text italic</em>`

178 HTML basics: headings

There are seven different types of headings ranging from h1 for a main heading, through h2, h3, all the way down to h7 for subheadings. In practice only the first three are commonly used. Type this to create a heading: **`<h1>Your heading here</h1>`**

179 HTML basics: images

An image tag needs a source ("src," the location of the image), width and height in pixels, and an alternative ("alt") text description of the image:

```
<img src="images/mypic.jpg" width="320"
height="240" alt="Me at the beach" />
```

180 HTML basics: links

A link has two parts; the visible part the user clicks on, and the location they will go to. Both are contained within an **<a>** tag. The "a" stands for "anchor."

```
<a href="http://www.jamiefreeman.co.uk">Visit my
page</a>
```

181 HTML basics: tables

Tables are for displaying tabular data, such as a list of prices and options. This simple example contains two rows ("tr") and two columns ("td"):

```
<table>
<tr>
<td>Item</td>
<td>Price</td>
</tr>
<tr>
<td>Widget</td>
<td>$100</td>
</tr>
</table>
```

182 Word is not web page software

Although Microsoft Word *can* create simple web pages, it's not really designed for that task. Your pages are unlikely to be web standards compliant, meaning they could trip some browsers up, be less accessible, and less visible to search engines.

183 Create HTML with any plain text editor

You can create HTML pages in any plain text editor, such as WordPad (Windows) or TextEdit (MacOS).

184 Avoid Word for HTML editing

Try to avoid using Microsoft Word to create or edit HTML pages. If the document formatting doesn't ruin your page, the spell checker won't know what to make of HTML tags! If you must use it, remember to save the files in Plain Text format.

185 Emergency HTML editing

If you need to edit some HTML and you don't have access to your usual HTML editor, remember that you can edit any HTML page using a plain text editor. It won't have the advantages of a dedicated package, but it will get the job done.

186 Separating style from content

Separate your style from your content using Cascading Style Sheets (CSS). This makes it much easier to make changes to the design of your website later on if you need to.

187 Class and id, what's the difference?

A class can be applied to any number of elements on a page, while an id can only be applied to a single element on a page.

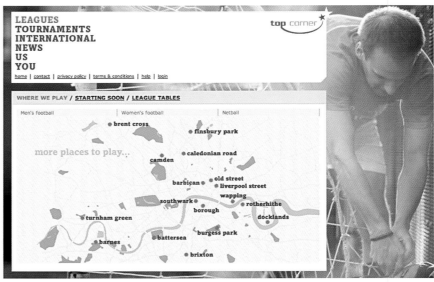

Caching

190 About your browser cache

Web browsers store files and images that you visit in order to display them more quickly the next time you ask for them. This causes problems for web designers because it can be unclear whether you are viewing the latest version or an older, "cached" version of a web page.

191 Cache confusion

Browser caching is a big source of confusion for clients during web development. They often ask why we haven't completed the changes they wanted, and the answer is usually that their browser is showing a "cached" version of the page!

192 Clear your cache

Get rid of your browser's stored copies of visited files to ensure it is displaying the latest version. You can do this by clearing your browser's cache, also known as "Temporary Internet Files."

193 Stop your browser from caching

When testing a site you can set your browsers' cache size to zero, effectively stopping it from storing local copies of web pages you visit. This will ensure you are always seeing the latest version of the sites you are developing.

194 Caching can be a good thing too

Don't forget that caching can be a good thing for general web surfing because it decreases the download time for previously visited pages. So don't forget to increase your cache size from zero once you've finished building your site.

188 How to code a CSS id

In your stylesheet you create an id like this:

#idName { attributes here }

Note the hash symbol before the id name.

189 How to code a CSS class

In your stylesheet you create a class like this:

.className { attributes here }

Note the period (full stop) before the class name.

195 Use "includes" to save time

If you find yourself adding the same content to multiple pages you should think about using "includes" to save time. By referencing a single chunk of code many times over you can make site-wide changes very easily. Common items like headers, footers, menus, etc. can all benefit from this technique.

196 A simple PHP include

You'll need to have PHP running on your server for this tip to work. Create a file named "footer.php" and enter this code into it:

```
<div id="footer">Website built by Jamie Freeman
2007</div>
```

Now open your web pages and paste the following code just before the closing **</body>** tag:

```
<?php include("footer.php"); ?>
```

The footer now appears on every page, so you only have to change it in one place for it to automatically update across the whole site.

197 Back up!

This is possibly the single most important tip in the book—if you spend weeks building a wonderful website it could all count for nothing if your hard disk goes belly up. Back up regularly to a safe medium that resides in a different location from your computer, such as a removable hard disk or CDR.

198 Backup media

A backup is simply a copy of your data, but there's no point copying it to the same disk that the original is on—if the disk dies then the back up is gone too. Back up on to external media. For example, you could back up on to CDRs, a removable USB drive, an iPod, or an external FireWire hard disk.

PayPal and eBay

201 Use PayPal to take payments online

Setting up PayPal for simple one-off payments is very easy and allows you to sell through your website. The service is highly professional and can be used by people without a PayPal account.

202 Customize your payment page

Change the look of your PayPal payment page to make it fit in with the rest of your site. Customers will feel more at home when paying and the site will seem more "trustworthy." Match the background color and place your logo at the top of the page.

203 Multiple PayPal payment pages

Not only can you customize the payment page, you can also set several up at the same time. This allows you to select different pages for different projects, but with all the payments going into the same account.

204 Use PayPal's shopping cart

Using PayPal's built-in cart is very straightforward, simply requiring some code to be pasted into your pages. Having a shopping cart will allow your customers to add multiple items and to pay once they have all the goods they want.

205 Use eBay to sell online

If setting up e-commerce on your website seems like a lot of hard work, why not use eBay instead? You can still have product descriptions on your main website, and these pages can simply link to your product on eBay. Check out eBay's "Buy Now" service, which may be more appropriate for your products than the usual auction method.

199 Back up frequently

The more frequently you back up, the less work you will lose in the event of a disaster. For example, if you back up weekly you could lose up to a week's worth of work. To decide how often you should back up, ask yourself this question: "How much work could I stand doing all over again?"

200 Rotate between two backups

As well as backing up frequently, you should also consider using a "rotating" strategy. For example, I use two portable FireWire hard disks for back up, which I swap over each week. That way I can revert to an older version of my work if I need to.

Two-column layouts

206 Use your Mac's built-in web server

If you use a Macintosh computer running OSX, you have a built-in web server right there! Put your websites into the Sites folder, then type this into your web browser, replacing "jamie" with your own user name:

localhost/~jamie

207 Test on multiple browsers

Remember to test your website on several different browsers, as they can look surprisingly different from one to another. Online services such as www.browsercam.com can help with this, or you can ask friends to check out your new site for you.

208 Two-column layout: step 1

This technique allows you to have a classic "menu on the left, content on the right" layout. Luckily, it's very easy to do. In your HTML page add two divs, like this:

<div id="col1"> Menu here </div>
<div id="col2"> Content here </div>

All of your menu content will go within the first div, and your main content will go within the second.

209 Two-column layout: step 2

Link a style sheet to your HTML page and create the basic styles. The bare minimum required is:

#col1 { float: left; width: 20%; }
#col2 { float: left; width: 80%; }

210 Two-column layout: step 3

The basic style controls the layout (e.g. the relative width of the columns) so now we'll augment that with some visual styles. For example, you could give the left-hand column (the "menu" area) a pale blue background by adding **background: #6CF;** within the col1 curly brackets.

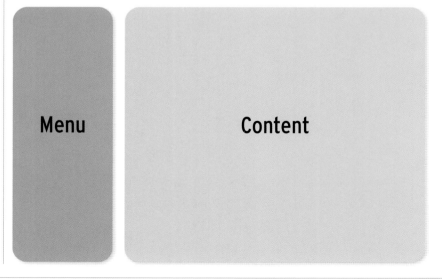

Menu   Content

Three-column layouts

211 Three-column layout: step 1

This technique is for creating pages with a left-hand menu, main content in the middle, and submenu on the right. The basics are simple, and follow on from the two column technique. This time you'll add an extra div into your page, like this:

<div id="col3"> Sub-menu here </div>

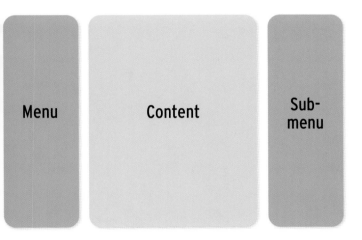

212 Three-column layout: step 3

You can make it easier to see what's going on in your layout by assigning colors or outlines to the three styles. For example, add **background: #333;** between the col1 and col3 curly brackets to put gray background on the outer columns.

213 Three-column layout: step 2

This time your style sheet will need three ids; one for each column. Both side columns will be 20 percent wide, adding up to 40 percent of the entire page width. That leaves 60 percent for the middle column, which is where your content will sit. Add the following into your linked CSS file:

#col1 { float: left; width: 20%; }
#col2 { float: left; width: 60%; }
#col3 { float: left; width: 20%; }

Batch processing

214 Batch processing images

When you have a lot of images to process (e.g. resize or convert to JPEG format) you should consider using batch processing techniques. They can take a bit of trial-and-error to master, but it's time well spent, especially if you have dozens of images to deal with.

215 Batch processing Photoshop

Photoshop has some extremely powerful batch processing techniques, although they can seem arcane at times. The basics are easy to understand though, and are based around "recording" the user's steps while they work on an image, allowing them to "replay" those same steps on another image. In the next few entries we'll walk through a common requirement—resizing a load of photographs and exporting them in JPEG format.

216 Batch processing Photoshop: step 1

As usual, preparation is everything. Start by putting all the images you want to process into a folder, called "originals." Create a folder next to it called "processed." Open one of the images in Photoshop and open the Actions tab, which you'll find under the Window menu.

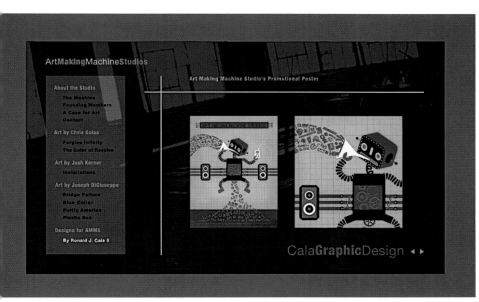

217 Batch processing Photoshop: step 2

In the Actions submenu select "New Action" and name it "Resize and JPEG." You'll see the "record" button has turned red, indicating that Photoshop will record (most) things you do until you press the square black "stop" button to its left.

218 Batch processing Photoshop: step 3

The first thing we want to do is resize the image. This is a common requirement because most digital cameras take photographs at a much higher resolution than you would typically display on a web page. Select Image Size from the Image menu and type in a width of 320 pixels and press the OK button. Notice that a new line (Image Size) has appeared in the Action window.

219 Batch processing Photoshop: step 4

Now select Save for Web in the File menu. (This option creates better-optimized JPEGs than the regular Save As command.) Select a compression level in the right-hand area of the screen, previewing the image to ensure it retains a reasonable level of quality.

220 Batch processing Photoshop: step 5

Press the Save button and in the following screen, navigate to the "processed" folder you created in step 1 and press Save again to put the new image in there. It will retain the same name (although the .jpg may be added if the original was in a different format) without fear of overwriting the original. That's why we created the new folder; it also allows you to return to the original if you are not happy with the results.

221 Batch processing Photoshop: step 6

Now close the image, but don't save it! Press the black square "stop" button at the bottom of the Actions tab, and that's the Action finished. You'll see another couple of lines under your action title now; Export and Close. (Clicking the little arrow to the left of each one reveals the details.)

222 Batch processing Photoshop: step 7

You now have an Action that you can apply to any image. Simply open an image, select your Action, and click the Play button. Magic! However, the real fun begins when you run the Action on a whole folder full of pictures, sitting back and relaxing while Photoshop tears through tons of photos that would take you all afternoon to do by hand! Start by selecting File > Automation > Batch.

223 Batch processing Photoshop: step 8

Choose your Action from the drop-down near the top of the resulting dialogue box, then select the "originals" directory as the Source folder. You may need to select "Suppress Color Profile Warnings," depending on how your system is configured.

224 Batch processing Photoshop: step 9

Choose the "processed" folder as the destination, and then look at the file naming options. This section allows you to apply some quite complex naming tricks if you require them, but we're going to use the same file names as the originals because we're saving into a different folder. Click the OK button and sit back...

225 Batch processing Photoshop: step 10

You should see your "processed" folder rapidly filling up with images as Photoshop does its thing. It will get through hundreds of images in minutes and it's a joy to watch all that hard work happening without you doing it! If the batch stops for some reason, step back through the process to figure out the problem. Bear in mind that I never got Actions and Batches to work correctly first time, so don't be too discouraged; it really is worth getting to grips with it.

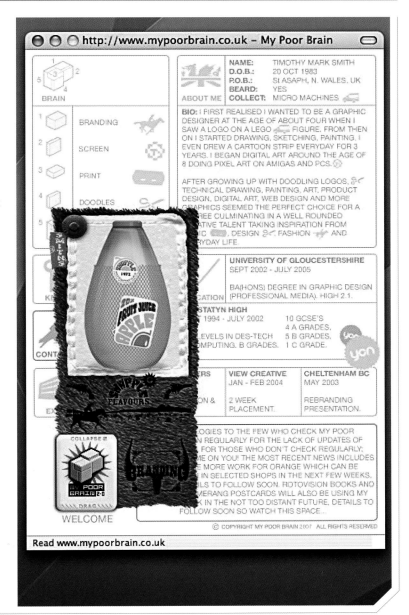

Hosting companies

226 Choosing a hosting company

Your website will need a webserver, and these are provided by hosting companies—they "host" your website on their servers. There are myriad companies offering all levels of service, but which one is right for you? Arm yourself with the following tips before you go looking for a home for your website.

227 Choosing a hosting company: 1

Hosting companies sometimes try to hide their technical support staff behind FAQ lists, contact forms, and even premium-rate phone numbers. You are likely to need help, especially when setting up your first website, so find out what level of support you can expect before you choose. It's worth paying a little bit more if it means you'll get better service.

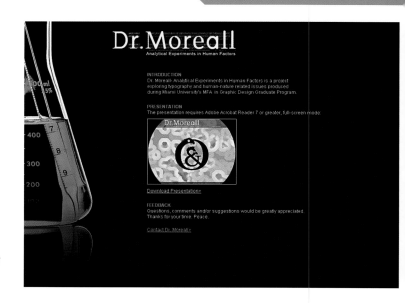

228 Choosing a hosting company: 2

Service levels range from "shared hosting," where your website sits on a computer with hundreds of thousands of others, to "dedicated hosting" where you have the entire server to yourself. Shared hosting is sufficient for the vast majority of sites, and is far more affordable. Dedicated servers are only required on extremely high-traffic sites, or those with specific technical or security issues that need addressing.

230 Choosing a hosting company: 4

The range of possible costs for web hosting is immense, going from free to—well, as much as you want to pay! Free services can be fine for simple, noncritical projects, but there are always restrictions or other downsides, such as bandwidth limits, high technical support costs, limited configuration options, and so on. Sometimes it pays to pay.

229 Choosing a hosting company: 3

Do you need a server for one site, or are you planning on making a number of sites? A "site" is usually defined by the fact that it has a unique domain name (e.g. www.message.uk.com), so you will need to check whether your package allows multiple domains if you plan to expand. If you're getting a hosting package for a client, a single domain is usually sufficient.

231 Choosing a hosting company: 5

Decide what you need and check the web host's list of features. If you're going to want to capture email addresses, or install a content management system, for example, you will need a database and scripting language. If not, you shouldn't be paying for features you won't use.

Code comments

232 Code comments

Leave notes in your HTML code as a way of describing what's going on, and making the code more orderly. For example, "This is where the image thumbnails go" or "Start of the footer section." These comments can be very helpful if you have to return to a page to edit it after a long time.

233 Code comments: a warning

Just because the browser doesn't render the HTML within comment tags doesn't mean they're totally invisible. Most web browsers allow the user to choose to "view source," and the comment codes will be visible to read. So be careful what you write in there!

234 Code comments: hiding code temporarily

Because any text within the comment tags will be hidden from the browser, you can use this instead of deleting chunks of code. For example, if you want to remove a feature from your page but you think you may need it again in the future, you can simply surround it with comment tags. Then, if you decide you want the feature back in, simply remove the tags.

235 Code comments: how-to

Adding a code comment is simple. All you have to do is surround the comment with these tags:

<!-- This is my comment. Hello world. -->

Any text within those tags will be ignored by the browser and will not display.

236 Code comments: take care with page structure

Take care that you start and end your comment codes in the right place. If you accidentally include a closing **</div>** or **</table>** tag within the comment you could disrupt the flow of the document and spoil the layout.

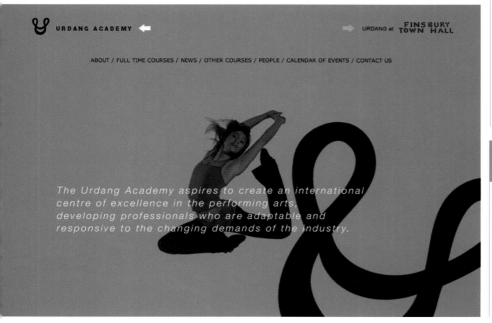

Custom bullet points

237 Custom bullet points: step 1

Let's get rid of those boring bullet points! The first thing to do is to design a replacement image. Don't forget that it still needs to work as a bullet point, so it should be quite bold, clear, and in proportion with your type size. When you've come up with a design, save it as a GIF called "bullet.gif" in your images folder.

- Potatoes
- Cabbage
- Sprouts

- ✹ Bananas
- ✹ Mangos
- ✹ Oranges

238 Custom bullet points: step 2

Assuming you have a style sheet linked to your HTML page, you just need to add a line of CSS code:

ul { list-style-image: url(images/bullet.gif); }

Test the page in your browser to see if the bullets line up properly.

239 Custom bullet points: step 3

If your bullets sit too high or low, the easiest way to fix the alignment is simply to add a couple of pixels at the top or bottom of the graphic. A bit of trial and error will soon get them aligned, but bear in mind that different font sizes on different computers will affect the alignment too.

240 Custom bullet points: step 4

If your bullet points might appear on different colored backgrounds (for example, you might have different colors for different site sections) then you should consider making the bullet as a transparent GIF.

241 Dividing page areas with lines

Rather than the simple blocks of color described in the two and three column layout techniques, you can create a smart, minimalist look by placing fine lines between the different page areas. On a white background a mid-gray, 1 pixel wide line looks great. Follow the next few tips to implement this.

242 Dividing page areas with lines: step 1

We'll apply this technique to the "header and footer" layout (see tip 259). Start by removing the background colors from all the styles. For example, your "head" style should change from this:

#head { width: 100%; background: #66CC00;} to this: **#head { width: 100%;}**

243 Dividing page areas with lines: step 2

The method for putting a line around a div is to give it a border style. CSS allows us to specify which side the border should be on. We don't need borders on every side of each div, so we'll proceed like this: the head will have a line at the bottom; col1 will have a line on the right, and foot will have a line at the top.

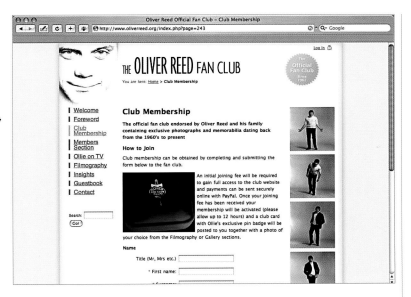

244 Dividing page areas with lines: step 3

Within the head style's curly brackets, add this text: **border-bottom: solid 1px #333;**. The first part defines which side of the div will be affected. The next part sets the style of the line. (Other options are "dashed" or "dotted," for example.) Then comes the width of the border (in pixels), and the last part gives it a color; gray in this case.

245 Dividing page areas with lines: step 4

Within the col1 style's curly brackets, add this text: **border-right: solid 1px #333;** Note that everything about this style is the same as before, except that the border part now applies the style to the right-hand edge of the div. You could have chosen to add the line to the left edge of the right-hand div, but you wouldn't need both. In this case I chose to add it to the right edge of the left-hand div.

246 Dividing page areas with lines: step 5

Within the foot style's curly brackets, add this text: **border-top: solid 1px #333;**. This creates a line above the footer. Another way of looking at this is as a line beneath the two columns above. Test the page in your browser and you should see two horizontal gray lines and one vertical, dividing the page into four sections.

247 Dotted lines

Using dotted lines to divide page areas gives a very technical feel to a page. Dotted lines can also be good for using around a call-out as it is reminiscent of real-world coupons or forms. Adding the following into a CSS style will add a dotted gray line around the element: **border: dotted 1px #333;**

Contact links

248 Easy contact link

The simplest way to allow people to email you through your site is to use the "mailto" link. Clicking the link will simply open up the user's default email application, with a new blank message addressed to them. Follow the next few tips to see how it's done.

249 Easy contact link: step 1

The mailto link is very similar to a regular hyperlink, and is created using the same **<a>** tag. First I'll show you what the completed link looks like, then we'll dissect it:

```
<a href="mailto:bob@message.uk.com">Email me</a>
```

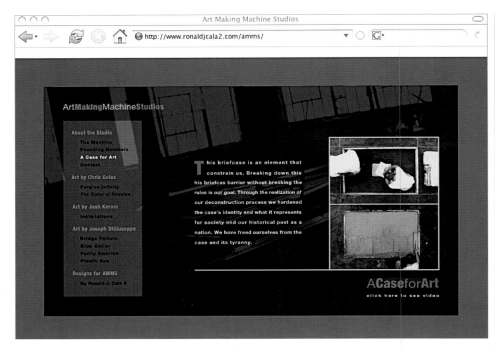

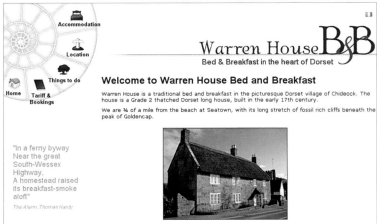

250 Easy contact link: step 2

Change **bob@message.uk.com** to the email address you want to use in your site. The text "Email me" is the link text; this is what the user will click on the page.

251 Easy contact link: step 3

You can extend this to include a subject line, giving your users even less to do (thus making it more likely they'll do it!). In this case you'll need to add **?subject=Email from your website** immediately after the email address. Would you like to have the email sent to multiple recipients? Read on...

252 Easy contact link: step 4

After the subject just add **&cc=info@message.uk.com** to have the email sent to another account. You can add more recipients if you need to. Just separate the list of recipients with commas, like this:

accounts@message.uk.com, sales@message.uk. com, janitor@message.uk.com

253 Easy contact link: step 5

Note that all recipients will be able to see all the email addresses the message is sent to. You might want to consider using "bcc" if this is more appropriate. As the users are likely to be in the same organization this is not likely to be a problem.

254 Easy contact link: step 6

Let's have a look at the entire code now:

```
<a href="mailto:bob@message.uk.
com?subject=Email from your website&cc=info@
message.uk.com, sales@message.uk.com">Email
me</a>
```

There's more...

255 Easy contact link: step 7

It is also possible to put in a message, perhaps to get people started. Add **&body=We love you Jamie!** (or whatever is appropriate!) into the string, straight after your final email address.

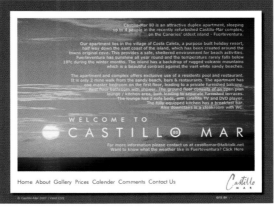

256 Fireworks HTML output

Fireworks can output HTML with quite sophisticated animation and rollover techniques, which makes it a tempting option for those who don't have great JavaScript or CSS skills. This can work quite successfully for very small sites with a high production value, but isn't really suitable for building larger sites.

257 Fireworks for prototyping

Even if you don't want to use Fireworks' HTML output capabilities for creating entire websites, it can still be useful for making quick prototypes. Your design visuals can easily be "sliced and diced" to give you a quick idea of how your site will feel, before you commit to building the whole thing.

258 Give divs semantic names

Give your divs and classes names that relate to the meaning of the content, not simply what they look like. This means that, when you come to redesign the site, you won't end up with a div called "redBox" that now displays in a shade of blue!

Header and footer layout

259 Header and footer layout

This series of techniques builds on the two and three column layouts by adding a header and footer. Headers typically contain "branding" such as logos, strap lines, etc., and sometimes contain the main navigation. Footers tend to contain additional navigation, copyright notices, technical information, and so on.

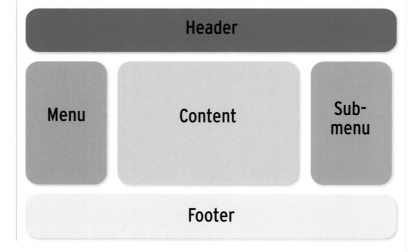

260 Header and footer layout: step 1

Start by following the two (or three) column layout technique. You should now have a simple HTML page that displays two colored columns side by side. Our first step is to add another two divs, above and below the columns. Type this directly before the col1 div:

```
<div id="head">Header content here</div>
```

261 Header and footer layout: step 2

If you test the previous step in your browser you should see some plain (i.e. unstyled) text above the two columns. This step adds some simple styling so you can see what's going on more clearly. Add this line in your style sheet and reload the page in your browser:

#head { width: 100%; background: #66CC00; }

262 Header and footer layout: step 3

You should now see a green box across the top of your page. This is the header. Adding the footer is just as easy. Type this at the end of your HTML file and reload your page in the browser:

<div id="foot">Footer content here</div>

263 Header and footer layout: step 4

The foot div requires some extra CSS to make it work properly as it follows on from two "floated" elements. It needs to sit under the columns, not float to the side, so we need to "clear" the preceding floats by adding **clear: both;** into the style. Here's how the whole line should look:

#foot { clear: both; width: 100%; }

264 Header and footer layout: step 5

Finally, give the footer a background color. Simply add this into the foot style to have a green background that matches the header style:

background: #66CC00;

265 Linking an external style sheet

Keep your styles separate from your HTML by linking to an external stylesheet. Type the following into the **<head>** element of your HTML page, replacing "mystyles.css" with the name of your stylesheet:

<link href="mystyles.css" rel="stylesheet" type="text/css">

Lists

266 Making unordered lists: step 1

W3C web standards-compliant lists are very simple to make. This technique is for unordered, or "bullet point," lists. Start by creating the container element, or **<ul>** tag, which stands for "unordered list." On two lines in your HTML page type the opening and closing tags:

```
<ul>
</ul>
```

267 Making unordered lists: step 2

Now that you have the container, it's time to put in some content. Each list item is surrounded by opening and closing "list item" tags, hence **<li>**. Type one line like the following for each item in your list:

```
<li>Collect laundry</li>
```

268 Making unordered lists: step 3

Keep adding list items until your list is complete and test it in your browser. Your list can contain links too. Simply add an **<a>** as you would for any link, but make sure it opens and closes within the **<li>** tags, like this:

```
<li>Call <a href="http://www.jamiefreeman.co.
uk">Jamie</a> re party</li>
```

269 Making unordered lists: step 4

Your complete list should look something like this:

```
<ul>
<li>Apples</li>
<li>Oranges</li>
<li>Mangoes</li>
</ul>
```

270 Making ordered lists: step 1

Ordered lists don't have bullet points. Instead, each item has a number. You don't have to type these numbers in though; HTML and your browser work out the numbers automatically. This is really useful, especially on longer lists, as it means you can slot new items into the list without having to renumber everything.

271 Making ordered lists: step 2

This technique is just like that for unordered lists, but we use a different tag to enclose the list. In HTML, this tag is referred to as an ordered list, hence **<ol>** Type in a pair of opening and closing tags, like this: **<ol></ol>**

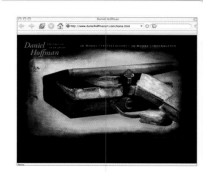

272 Making ordered lists: step 3

As with unordered lists, you need to add the list items within the **<ol>** tags, each within their own **<li>** tags. Ordered lists use the same list item tag as unordered lists; it's the enclosing **<ol>** tag that defines it as "ordered."

273 Making ordered lists: step 4

Adding the list items is identical to the technique for making unordered lists. It's really important to remember not to type in the numbers though, as the browser will automatically put numbers in. If you do, you'll end up with a list that looks like this:
1. 1. Get cape
2. 2. Wear cape
3. 3. Fly!

274 Making ordered lists: step 5

Your formatted ordered, or "numbered," list should look like this:

```
<ol>
<li>Boil kettle</li>
<li>Make tea</li>
<li>Dip cookie</li>
</ol>
```

Test it in your browser to see the numbers magically appear!

275 Nested lists

Now that you've got the hang of lists, let's mix it up a bit! Say you have an ordered list of cookery instructions. You might get to a particular step and wish to insert a sublist of ingredients. The following tips will help you create quite complex documents, which are especially useful for presenting complicated technical information.

276 Nested lists: step 1

Create an ordered list with three items, like this:

```
<ol>
<li>Print invitations</li>
<li>Invite guests</li>
<li>Party!</li>
</ol>
```

277 Nested lists: step 2

It's an ordered list in this example because the steps have to be carried out in a certain sequence, but the technique works for unordered lists too. The next step is to create a sublist of guests to invite. As there's no specific order in which to invite the guests the sublist can be unordered:

```
<ul>
<li>Ben</li>
<li>Laura</li>
<li>Tim</li>
<li>Martin</li>
</ul>
```

278 Nested lists: step 3

Use cut-and-paste to move the list you just created into the ordered list. Place your cursor after the closing **</li>** tag following the list item "Invite guests" and type in a return to create a new line. Paste the list of guests in, and open the page in your browser. You should see a list that looks like this:

1. Print invitations
2. Invite guests
   - Ben
   - Laura
   - Tim
   - Martin
3. Party!

279 Preview your work regularly

The more often you preview your page in a web browser, the fewer steps you'll have to retrace when something goes wrong.

280 Easy previewing

Keep a web browser open with your page already loaded. Then you can simply toggle between your web design software and the browser, and hit "refresh" whenever you want to check your progress.

281 Save time typing code

HTML tags are contained within pairs of angle brackets. Type the two angle brackets at the same time, then use your back arrow to place the cursor between them, ready to type in the content of the tag. You'll be amazed how much time this can save!

Show your work online

282 Simple HTML portfolio

A great way to show your design work or photographs is to create an online portfolio. The portfolio could be a small site, or part of a larger one. It should be easy to use, and preferably easy for you to update too. Work through the following tips to create a simple HTML-based portfolio.

283 Simple HTML portfolio: step 1

Each page will be an HTML file containing an image, title, caption, and navigation. The first step is to create a basic HTML page; use your editing software to create a blank page, and give it a title, such as "Jamie Freeman: Portfolio." This will appear in the browser header and will also show up in search engine results, so make sure it's meaningful. Save the file as portfolio_X.htm.

284 Simple HTML portfolio: step 2

Now we're going to put in the basic heading, image, and caption. Add this text between the opening and closing **<body>** tags:

```
<h1>Image 1</h1>
<img src="images/image_1.jpg" alt="Image description" width="640" height="480">
<p>Image caption</p>
```

285 Simple HTML portfolio: step 3

To navigate between the pages we'll need to add some links. In this case, we'll have text links saying "Previous" and "Next," separated by a "pipe" symbol (a vertical bar). Add the following code after the **<p>** tag from the previous step:

```
<p>
<a href="portfolio_X.htm">Previous</a> |
<a href="portfolio_X.htm">Next</a>
</p>
```

Don't worry, we're going to replace those X's later on.

286 Simple HTML portfolio: step 4

You now have the basic HTML template for your entire portfolio, so check it in the browser before you move on. Make sure you're happy with this page as you are soon going to have a lot of similar pages, so amends will be much easier to make at this stage.

287 Simple HTML portfolio: step 5

Now you need to prepare your images. Crop them to 640 x 480 pixels for this example (as specified in the **<img>** tag in step 2) and save as JPEG files in a directory called images. This directory should sit alongside your HTML file. Name them image_1.jpg, image_2.jpg, and so on.

292 Simple HTML portfolio: step 10

On the last page there is no need for a next link, so simply delete the line. Now is a good time to run through the entire portfolio, checking the navigation on all pages, in both directions.

288 Simple HTML portfolio: step 6

Duplicate the HTML file and call the new copy index.htm. This is the first page users will see. Change the text within the **<h1>** tag to the name of the first image. The image will be correctly named in this first page, but you'll need to edit the alt text to accurately describe the image. Lastly, edit the caption.

290 Simple HTML portfolio: step 8

Duplicate portfolio_X.htm again, and rename it portfolio_2.htm. Edit the heading, image, alt text, and caption as before. (The image will be images/image_2.jpg this time.) The first link should read **<a href="index.htm">Previous</a>** as it will lead to the first page in the portfolio. The second link will go to portfolio_3.htm, so edit the next line accordingly.

293 Target JPEG sizes

There are no hard-and-fast target image sizes, but it's good to have an idea of what to expect. The following table is only a guide, as the actual results are dependent on the image content:

Pixel size	File size
800 x 600	45k
640 x 480	30k
320 x 240	10k
120 x 90	3k

289 Simple HTML portfolio: step 7

As this is the first page in your portfolio there will not be a "previous" image, so we need to remove that link. Simply delete the whole line, including the "pipe" at the end. The next page in the portfolio will be called portfolio_2.htm so edit the next line to read

<a href="portfolio_2.htm">Next</a>.

291 Simple HTML portfolio: step 9

Repeat step 8 for as many pages as you want in your portfolio, always checking the previous and next links go to the correct pages before and after the one you're currently editing. Check the pages in your browser each time you've edited them. In this example, we'll have 10 pages, so when you get up to portfolio_10.htm you'll need to go on to the next step.

Accessibility and Web

Inclusive web design

Web accessibility is the practice of making sure your website content can be accessed and understood by as many people as possible, regardless of their physical ability. A typical example is that of users with visual impairment, such as color blindness or shortsightedness. But other conditions such as reduced motor function or learning difficulties can also come into play. It may not always be possible to make all types of content accessible to all people, but as far as possible you should try to make the meaning of your content understood by everyone.

294 What are web standards?

This topic crops up in quite a few places in this book! The reason is simply that web standards are incredibly useful and important. They help to ensure compatibility between different computer systems and browser versions, as well as aiding accessibility and search engine optimization.

295 Find out more about web standards

The place to go for definitive information about web standards is the website of the group responsible for setting them, the World Wide Web Consortium, or W3C for short: www.w3.org.

Standards

296 Halfway to accessibility

The beauty of coding to W3C web standards is that you'll find your sites are already well on the way to being accessible. In fact, a simple site properly coded will require very little special attention to bring it up to the highest level of accessibility.

297 Good contrast for your text

Make sure that your text contrasts well with the background color, otherwise it will be hard for some people to read easily. You might feel pale gray looks very cool, but spare a thought for people without 20/20 vision!

That's all very well if you have 20-20 vision

but it's best to ensure your text is easy to read

298 Alt text

Use the alt attribute to describe the content of images for visually impaired users. Some people use screen reader software which reads the text content of web pages using speech synthesis. If your images have no alt text then the meaning of such images will not be available to them.

299 Alt text for "eye candy" images

If an image is simply there as eye candy—in other words, it is attractive but conveys no particular meaning—you should still use the alt attribute. But in this case it should be set to "null" like this:

```
<image src="images/fancy_pattern.jpg" alt="">
```

300 Avoid drop-down menus

Why don't Amazon, MSN, eBay, Yahoo!, etc., use drop-down menu systems? It's not because they don't know how! It's more likely that they know through extensive user testing that drop-down menus just aren't great for users, no matter how cool designers think they look.

301 Don't say "bold," say "strong"

Rather than put a "bold" tag around your text use the standards-compliant form "strong." By default, this will display as bold text in the browser. It also allows a speech reader to interpret such text differently; by a change of tone for example.

\<strong\>Hello world\</strong\>

302 Improve browser compatibility

Making sure your website is coded to W3C web standards ensures it will be compatible with the widest possible range of web browsers.

303 New window warning

If your link is going to open a new browser window then don't forget to warn users what is about to happen. Some people can be disorientated by a new browser window springing up, so add some text like "Link opens a new window" in brackets after your link text.

304 Opening up creative possibilities

Coding to web standards isn't all about accessibility and compatibility; it also opens up great creative benefits. For example, you can override default browser styles such as **\<strong\>** tags appearing as bold text. Why not have them appear as if they have been highlighted?

305 Self-closing tags

Remember to "self-close" tags where appropriate. For example, to add a new line in a paragraph you could just add an old-style "break" tag: **\<br\>** However, the standards-compliant version of the tag self-closes, like this: **\<br /\>**

ALICE IN WONDERLAND

'Alice's Adventures In Wonderland' is probably the first real children's novel. Until Lewis Carroll came along, it was practically unheard of for a publisher to release a book that aimed to give pleasure and entertainment to children with no secret educational or moral motives. But Carroll and 'Alice' changed all that.

© TopFoto.co.uk

But who was he, this Oxford mathematician, and how did he come to write this classic work? And what is its legacy? If there had been no Alice, would we really have no Winnie-the-Pooh, no Roald Dahl, Peter Pan? Would we never have met Frodo and Gollum, or had exciting adventures at Hogwarts? And what do people think of Alice today, a century and a half since it was first published?

YOU ARE IN : Home > The ICONS > Our Collection > Alice In Wonderland

ABOUT THIS ICON
→ ALICE IN WONDERLAND
+ BIOGRAPHY
+ FEATURES
+ WHAT'S NEXT
+ NEWS

RELATED ICONS

SEE RELATED ICONS

BIOGRAPHY

Read about how 'Alice in Wonderland' came to be written, how it changed the tradition of children's story-telling, and the versions that have been made of it since its first success.

READ THE ALICE BIOGRAPHY

FEATURES

Come on a journey into the Victorian world, meet some inspired inventors, and look at the work of some of the illustrators who have followed in the footsteps of Sir John Tenniel. We talk to Marina Warner about fairy-stories, and Jonathan Miller about his own film adaptation of 'Alice'.

SEE FEATURES

NOMINATE

"_Mini Cooper has always been dear to my heart..._"
MARK TOMPKINS

NOMINATE AN ICON

---

306 Site maps

A site map can be a great aid to accessibility, not just for disabled people, but also for anyone having trouble navigating your site. It should be simple, clear, and text-based—a simple indented list is best. For example:

Products
- Widgets
- Gadgets

Services
- Catering
- Entertainment

About us
- Where we are
- Contact us

307 Reasonable text size

It can be tempting to make the text on your site very small; it looks modern and neat. But if you want to make your site accessible, you must use a reasonable text size in order to accommodate users with less than perfect vision.

309 Provide text resizing links

In addition to allowing users to override your font sizes, you can go one step farther by actually providing links allowing them to do it. This works by having two or more style sheets, which are swapped using a JavaScript when the appropriate link is clicked.

308 Resizeable text

Write your CSS so that the user can override your text size. Use relative units of measure such as "ems" rather than pixels.

310 Get help from GAWDS

If you are committed to producing web designs that can be accessed by the widest possible group of people, regardless of physical ability, consider joining the Guild of Accessible Web Designers (www.gawds.org). It can offer resources, loads of excellent examples, and a community of like-minded people to provide help and support. (Some of the examples shown in this book are by GAWDS members.)

311 Automated accessibility validation

There are several online accessibility validators, perhaps the best known of which is "Bobby." You can get these to check over pages in your site, and they will list all the problems they find. Visit webxact.watchfire.com.

312 A note about accessibility validation

The list of errors and warnings the automated services display can be alarmingly long, but fear not. The validator is not able to accurately assess all accessibility issues, so the list will contain lots of things it thinks might be a problem, which you will have to check manually.

313 How accessibility levels work

There are three levels of accessibility, defined by the Web Accessibility Initiative in the Web Content Accessibility Guidelines (WCAG). Sites are judged against these in terms of "conformance" to certain levels, of which there are three: A, AA, and AAA, which range from basic to advanced accessibility. More information is available here: www.w3.org/WAI

314 PAS 78

This Publicly Available Specification serves as a guide to clients for commissioning websites, and is recommended reading for anyone who takes the provision of accessible websites seriously. More information is available at www.message.uk.com/index.php?page=41 and you can download the document from www.drc-gb.org.

315 Alternative content for Flash

Flash content can be made accessible using later versions of the program but there are still good reasons for providing such content in an alternative format. If the core meaning of your SWF can be described in words, offer users a link to a text version of the file.

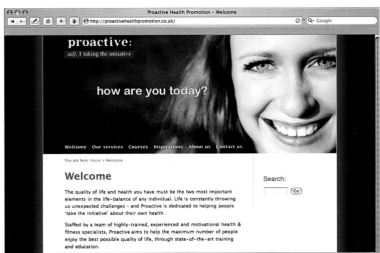

Semantic markup

316 Semantic markup

"Semantic markup" is the technique of writing HTML code that describes the meaning of the content, rather than simply describing its layout or style. This allows both human readers (e.g. fellow web developers) and machines (e.g. Google) to read and understand the context of the content. This context gives the content an extra layer of meaning. The following few examples should help you understand the simple power behind the semantic web.

317 Semantic markup: example 1

One of the most important examples, in my opinion, is that of the **<h1>** tag, which contains the main heading of the page. Everything else on the page is subordinate to the main heading. Put another way, the main heading is the most important thing on the page. Knowing this allows search engines to view the contents of the heading accordingly, and give those keywords extra weight when deciding the page's rank.

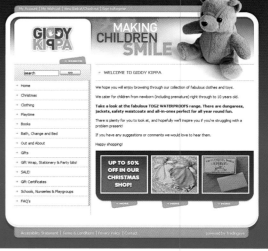

318 Semantic markup: example 2

If the main heading is the most "important" content on the page, and if everything else is subordinate to it, then it follows that there can only be one **<h1>** on a given page. Opinion differs on this, and I would accept that certain conditions might apply to make two "main" headings acceptable, but in the vast majority of cases, your pages should only have one.

319 Semantic markup: example 3

If your page requires further headings, subordinate to the main one, then you should put in second-level headings using the **<h2>** tag. If within these subheadings, you require further headings you can use **<h3>**. Subdivisions within another section would use **<h4>**, and so on. In practice, I have never once required a fourth level heading, but you might find them useful if working with highly complex academic or legal content. The number of HTML headings goes all the way to seven.

320 Semantic markup: example 4

Remember that using these tags has nothing to do with what they look like—it's all about what they mean. However, all browsers will have default display styles for these and other standard HTML tags. Don't, under any circumstances, use a heading tag simply to make text look bigger or bolder. If your text is a heading to the text that follows it, use an "h" tag.

321 Semantic markup: example 5

The key to semantic markup is to make use of the existing classes provided within the HTML specification. This also saves you a lot of time! If you do need to represent something in a visually different manner you can still do this by adding a custom "class" to the standard tag, like this: **<p class="sales-page">**, and creating a corresponding style in your CSS.

322 Semantic markup: example 6

A subtle, but instructive, piece of semantic markup is the **<strong>** tag. Most of the time this is used to make the text bold. So why not use the old **<b>** tag? Well, for one thing, it's not web standards-compliant. More pertinently, it is a "representational" tag, meaning it only refers to the way the content should look, rather than what it means. **<strong>** means that the content is "prominent," a concept which could be represented in any way you wish, not necessarily bold.

323 Semantic markup: example 7

Similar to the **<strong>** tag is the **<em>** tag. Again, this is mostly used to denote italic text, which used to be accomplished with the nonstandard **<i>** tag. The semantic meaning of **<em>** is "emphasis," whereas **<i>** just means "slopey text." The fact that some text is "sloping" means nothing to a blind person or a search engine. That it has "emphasis" means a lot. For the design savvy among us, there are lots of ways to give emphasized text a visual representation other than italicizing it.

324 Semantic markup: example 8

Tables are another area where the meaning of HTML markup is often sacrificed for the designer's convenience. Semantically, a "table" is a matrix of related data organized into rows and columns, like a list of product names with associated prices and color options for example. Tables shouldn't be used for creating layouts, as the fact that it's a "table" implies a structured relationship between items in the rows and columns that doesn't exist.

325 Semantic markup: example 9

Let's not forget the humble "paragraph" tag, known as **<p>** to his friends. The paragraph is to a document as the brick is to a wall. So whatever you do, don't just chuck in **
** tags to create the visual appearance of paragraphs; something that many web designers seem to do with alarming frequency. That would be like building a wall with no cement. If you need more space between your paragraphs, look to your CSS and make the changes there, not in your document.

326 Semantic markup: example 10

If you code your page semantically before embarking on the styling, you will have created a small, perfectly-formed HTML document that all users, browsers, search engines, and speech readers will be able to understand. Now you can get into what it looks like, for those who can see it.

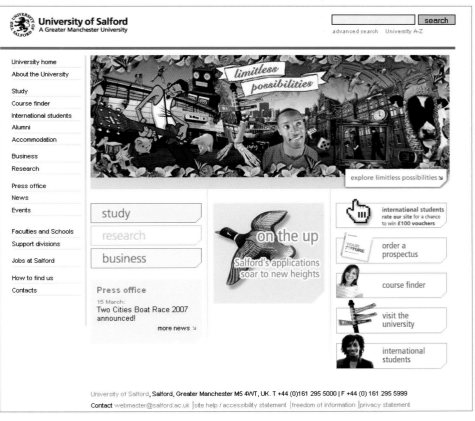

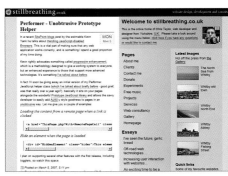

Getting Found

Search engines
One of the most important aspects of web design is making sure your website can be easily found. Eighty-five percent of all browsing sessions begin with a web search. This section will explain how you can make sure that your site is visible.

327 Search Engine Optimization (SEO)

This is the process of analyzing every single aspect of your website from the point of view of how it performs in search engines. Accommodating search engines is extremely important, but SEO should be done without any detrimental effect on the experience of real users.

328 Types of search engine

There are two main types of search engines; directories and "crawlers." Directories (e.g. Yahoo!) are compiled by human researchers, so when you use them you're actually searching their directory, not the whole web. Crawler-based services (e.g. Google) use software "spiders" to "crawl" the web, automatically cataloging sites as they go.

329 Don't try to trick Google

Google has a huge team of developers and a budget of millions of dollars. Do you really think you're smarter than them? No, I thought not. Don't try to trick the search engines into giving you a better search results placing—if they think you are trying "spamming" techniques you will be penalized for it. Your site could take many months to get back up the rankings.

330 Alt text makes images visible to search engines

Search engines can't "see" images, so make sure important information that sighted users get from an image is embedded in the alt text. This is especially important when you are using graphics for headings and text.

331 Alt text for graphical text

If you are using graphics for headings, make sure the alt text is identical to that used in the graphic. If you don't, then search engines (and nonsighted users) are likely to misunderstand the meaning of your pages.

332 Understanding alt text

Alt text is designed for a specific task: to describe the meaning of an image to a person or machine that can't see it. Bear that in mind when you write your alt texts and you won't go far wrong.

333 Don't abuse the alt text attribute

Don't try to fool search engines by filling alt text with spurious keywords as this type of "spamming" causes serious accessibility problems.

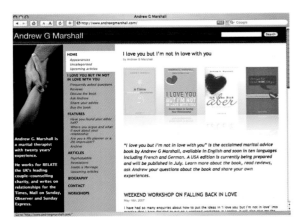

334 Check your spelling

Make sure you spell check your website text, otherwise important keywords might not get found in web searches.

Using Google

335 Google tips

It's a good idea to increase your knowledge of how Google works in order to help improve your search engine ranking. Becoming better at searching will help you understand how to tweak your site for search engine friendliness!

336 Google tips 1: localization

Google detects your location before deciding which version of its site to show you. Even if you type in google.com you might end up being shown google.co.uk, for example. However, the results will still be delivered from the main directory, unless you specifically choose "pages from the UK."

337 Google tips 2: exact phrase

If you searched Google for Jamie Freeman you would get over 12 million results, as it looks for every instance of both words. You can target your search by looking for an *exact phrase*. Do this by putting quote marks around your search term, e.g. "Jamie Freeman," and it will only find pages that match that phrase exactly.

338 Google tips 3: site search

Google doesn't have to search the entire web; you can just search a particular website. For example, you could find articles about accessibility on my company's website by typing in the search term (i.e. "accessibility") followed by the word "site," a colon, then the full URL for the site you want to search. Like this: accessibility site:http://www.message.uk.com.

339 Google tips 4: who links to you?

You can find out which other sites have links to yours by typing the word "link" followed by a colon and your URL, like so: link:www.message.uk.com. Google only lists sites with a relatively high Page Rank however, so not all your in-bound links will appear. (www.alltheweb.com has a similar function which doesn't rely on Page Rank.)

340 Take misspellings and variations into account

Including common misspelt versions of words and spelling variations (e.g. theater and theatre) on your site means you might just pick up some extra visitors, but make it clear you know they are misspelt, or you could end up looking stupid.

341 Relevant content

The absolute number one thing your website needs for good search engine performance is relevant content. If your site is not about what it claims to be about then no amount of other tips and techniques will help you. (Even if people do find your site they are likely to be annoyed if they find irrelevant content.)

342 Clean and lean code

Search engines take notice of the HTML code that makes up your page. The more code there is relative to the amount of actual content, the worse your site will perform in search engine rankings.

343 Google is a "blind user"

A side effect of creating accessible websites is that they are naturally very well suited to good search engine optimization. There is a saying in the web accessibility world that "Google is the web's biggest blind user," and the meaning is simple: Google and other search engines can't "see" images, colors, styling, etc., so ensure the meaning of such elements is also available in text format.

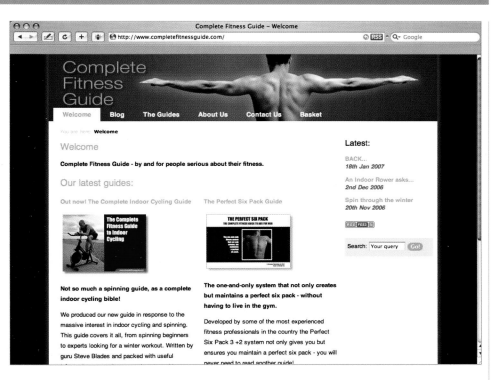

344 Standards compliance

If your website is coded to comply with W3C web standards it is more likely to perform well in search engine results. The reason for this is simply that they are less likely to "trip up" on some code they don't understand.

345 Headings and subheadings

If you put a main heading on your page it should be enclosed by an **<h1>** tag. This tells the browser that it is a level one heading. Subheadings would use **<h2>**, **<h3>**, etc. This markup helps search engines know which are the most important pieces of text on a page.

346 In-bound links

Links to your site from external websites are very important for search engine optimization. Not only do they help the search engine find your site in the first place, they can also improve the ranking your site achieves. If a large number of sites with related content link to you, the search engines will look upon you favorably.

347 Use your sites to boost each other

If you have several sites you can use each of them to improve the search engine ranking of the others. Create links on each site to all the other sites. It helps if the content on each site is somehow related.

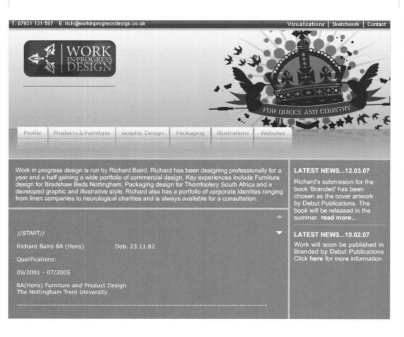

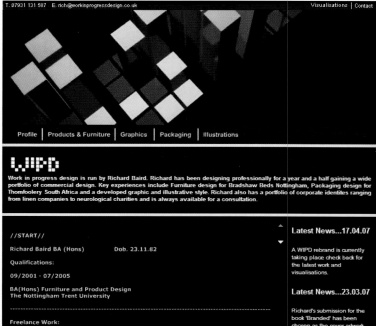

348 Get your friends to help

If you have friends with their own websites (for example MySpace or Blogger pages), ask them if they will put a link to your site on theirs.

349 Search engines need text!

Without text, search engines have nothing to get their teeth into. Make sure your site has plenty of text content, even if it's based around Flash or images. For example, make good use of alt text for images, and put text content in the HTML page that contains your SWF files.

350 The "Holy Trinity" of SEO

Remember, to achieve good search engine results you need just three things:
- Relevant text content
- Clean, standards-compliant code
- In-bound links

It's so simple it's a wonder everyone doesn't do it!

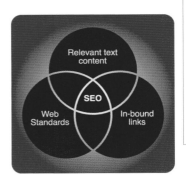

351 Identifying search terms

Start by considering the sort of terms people would type into a search engine to find a site like yours. For example, if you have a site about Country music they would be likely to type things like "country," "bluegrass," and so on.

352 Implementing search terms

Once you've decided on a core set of search terms, you need to ensure that they occur in your pages. For example, if your Country music website referred to "indigenous American music" you might want to replace that wording with "Country and Bluegrass music."

353 Don't abuse keywords

Trying too hard can often bring down the wrath of the search engines. If you swamp your page with keywords (e.g. repeating "widget" 500 times) then you are far more likely to harm your rankings than improve them as the search engines will regard this as "spamming."

354 Don't try too hard

When I bought my beautiful Martin acoustic guitar some time ago I wrote a blog post about it. Within a fortnight, my page was coming second only to the manufacturer's site when I did a Google search on the term "Martin acoustic." The moral of this story is that I didn't make any extra effort to achieve this result; I simply wrote the article as normal, in a clean, lean, standards-compliant website.

355 Feeding the spiders

An illustrator friend of mine (www.altar-image.com) describes search engine optimization like this: "The search engines send out spiders to hunt on the web. What they want is a diet of relevant text content. Once you understand what they eat, all you have to do is feed them." I couldn't have put it better myself.

356 The "meta" tag

There is actually only one **\<meta\>** tag, but it gets referred to a lot in relation to search engine optimization—erroneously for the most part—simply as "meta tags." For example, "meta description" is the **\<meta\>** tag with a name attribute of "description." It looks like this: **\<meta name="description"\>**

357 Meta description

The meta description has some use in search engine optimization, but it won't actually help improve your ranking. Its usefulness lies in the fact that some search engines (Google included) display the description in its search results. This allows you to create a very targeted piece of text, rather than just letting the search engine grab the chunk of text from your page that just happens to include the searched term.

358 Keywords in meta description

Although the meta description will not in itself improve your rankings, there's still a reason to include keywords (i.e. words people are likely to search for that relate to your site) in the description. Google and other search engines highlight the search terms in the description display and this can reinforce the impression that your page contains what they're after.

359 Meta keywords

Meta keywords was designed to allow you to provide additional text information for crawler-based search engines. However, these days virtually all search engines ignore the tag; the consensus is that it's not worth bothering with.

360 What is a keyword?

In relation to search engines, these are simply the words (or phrases) that the user is searching for. If the keywords occur in your pages you stand a good chance of turning up in the search engine results for that particular search. If they don't, you won't. Simple!

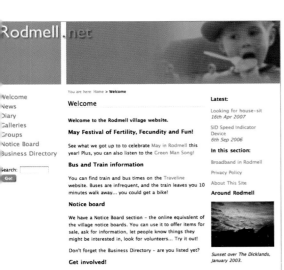

361 What is "keyword density?"

This phrase refers to an "optimum" ratio of search terms (i.e. phrases people are likely to be searching for) to page content. If your text has a good smattering of such words or phrases you will be looked upon kindly by the search engines.

362 Optimum keyword density

Unfortunately there's no such thing; or if there is no-one outside Google knows the formula! As ever, my advice here is to take a common sense approach, and always write your copy for human readers first and foremost. So, if your site sells widgets, it makes good sense to ensure that the word widget appears several times—but not too often!—in your pages.

363 Use page-specific meta descriptions

Create a page-specific meta description for each page in your site and you might just encourage a few extra clicks when your page comes up in a search engine listing. Make sure the text adequately describes the page contents, and what the user will find there.

Cool Stuff

Advanced web design
Spice up your website with some of these more advanced techniques and simple tips to make your site more professional, better looking, more engaging, and more fun!

364 Flash versions

Some 96 percent of browsers are able to display some form of Flash content. However, the latest version of the plug-in is only installed on 25-40 percent of browsers. Bear this in mind when deciding which version to output, and opt for older versions where your content allows.

365 Checking for the Flash plug-in

When you export your Flash movie you can opt to check that the user has the appropriate plug-in. This creates a JavaScript to check the user's browser, and if they do not have the correct version they can be offered alternative content such as a static JPEG.

366 Not everyone has Flash

While the majority of web browsers do have the Flash plug-in installed, there are still plenty of people who don't use it. With current estimates of internet user numbers topping 800 million worldwide, even a small percentage without Flash adds up to many millions of users.

367 Embedding small Flash objects

Flash doesn't have to comprise your entire website. You can use small Flash objects to accomplish specific tasks, such as adding an animated menu, a banner advert, or simply to add some eye-candy.

368 Keep track of visitor numbers

Keep track of the number of people visiting your site—as well as which pages are most popular—by using one of the many web statistics programs. It will also give you useful information such as where the visitors came from and how long they spent looking at your site.

369 Google Analytics

Google offers a web statistics program called Analytics. It's easy to install and offers some of the most detailed analysis of website traffic available. It's free, easy to implement, and incredibly useful.

370 Installing Google Analytics

Sign up for a free Google Analytics account, then paste the small piece of code they provide into every page you wish to track, just before the closing **</body>** tag. Go back to the Analytics page to check the installation has worked, and wait 24 hours to start to see useful data.

371 Creating "highlighted" text

Create a style to turn bold text into a highlighter effect by adding this to your stylesheet:

```
strong { background-color: #FFFF00; }
```

372 Simple bevelled panels

Create a simple bevel effect around colored panels with this snippet of CSS:

```
.panel {
border-top: 2px solid #E3E3E3;
border-left: 2px solid #E3E3E3;
border-right: 2px solid #666;
border-bottom: 2px solid #666;
background: #CCC; }
```

Now add the appropriate div around the content you want to appear on a panel:

```
<div class="panel">Hello</div>
```

373 Targeting your styles

"Nest" styles within one another to control where they are applied. For example, wrap a div around your menu (**<div id="menu">**) then create a style called **#menu a** and give it some properties, like **font-weight: bold;** Your menu links will appear in bold text, while others remain unaffected.

374 White photo-style borders

Create a style that mimics the white borders of a photographic print. Add this style to your CSS:

```
.photo { border: 4px solid #FFF; }
```

Now add the class "photo" to all the photographs on your pages:

```
<img src="images/holiday.jpg" class="photo" />
```

375 Opening a new window

You can make a link open a new browser window by adding a "target" parameter to your code, like this:

```
<a href="http://www.message.uk.
com" target="_blank">Click
Here!</a>
```

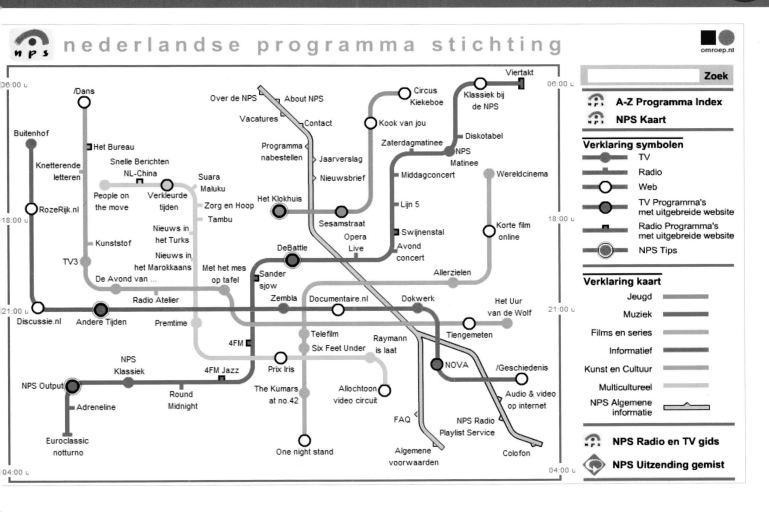

376 Add Google search to your website

Google doesn't just search the entire web, you can also get it to act as a search just for your own site. You will need a Google account, then visit www.google.com/coop and follow the simple instructions. Within a few minutes you'll have all the power of Google on your own site.

Adding Flash

377 Adding Flash to your pages

There are two ways to add Flash files (or more correctly, SWF files) to your HTML pages. Firstly, the Flash application itself has plenty of Export options, and these are probably the best place to start. The second method allows you to place minimal, standards-compliant code directly into your HTML page. This method is probably more flexible and is suitable for most applications.

378 Adding Flash manually

The Export techniques do have some advantages, especially for the newcomer. But this technique covers virtually all eventualities and has some advantages of its own. Not least of these is that it uses a very small amount of standards-compliant code, and requires no browser scripting. It's also very easy to understand and is great for placing a Flash file just where you want it.

379 Adding Flash manually: step 1

Rather than Export the SWF from Flash, you will simply select Test Movie from the Control menu. This creates a file with the same name as your Flash file, but with the .swf suffix. Copy this file to the "images" directory of your site.

380 Adding Flash manually: step 2

Next, you'll need the code. Type this into your HTML page:

```
<object type="application/x-shockwave-flash"
data="images/portfolio.swf" width="640"
height="480">
<param name="movie" value="images/portfolio.
swf" />
<img src="portfolio.jpg" width="640"
height="480" alt="Sorry, you can't view my Flash
portfolio." />
</object>
```

381 Adding Flash manually: step 3

Within that block of code you should be able to easily spot the parts you are likely to need to edit, including the name of the SWF as well as its pixel dimensions. If you followed the steps to create a simple Flash portfolio then the chances are your HTML will work without any alterations.

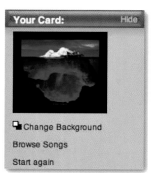

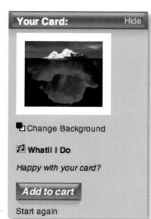

382 Adding Flash manually: step 4

As well as embedding the Flash file, the code also includes a regular **<img>** tag within the **<object>** tag. You need to create a JPEG or GIF image that will be displayed in the event that the user doesn't have the Flash plug-in installed. This would normally be a representative still image from the movie.

383 Adding Flash manually: step 5

Finally, edit the alt text for the **<img>** tag. This is an accessibility requirement to accommodate users who can't see the replacement image. Don't forget, this includes search engines such as Google, so make sure the text you enter here is a good description of the content of the image and the Flash file.

Exporting Flash

384 Exporting Flash to HTML: step 1

Explore Flash's Edit menu and you'll see the Publish Settings option. Select this, and in the Formats tab choose Flash and HTML. This will output an HTML page with the code in place to import your movie.

385 Exporting Flash to HTML: step 2

The Flash tab contains options for compression settings and Audio quality. Leave these at the defaults, or experiment with them—especially if you need to get the file size down.

386 Exporting Flash to HTML: step 3

The HTML tab is the most pertinent one for our purposes, and also the most complicated! Luckily, the Template options come with some descriptions next to the selector. It's a good idea to use one of the detection methods on offer, as these will handle those (few) users who do not have the Flash plug-in installed.

387 Exporting Flash to HTML: step 4

Sometimes, of course, you might just want to have the Flash file appear as a small part of an existing web page. In that case, you should be able to use the appropriate Export option, then simply copy the Flash-related code from the page Flash has created, and paste it into your existing HTML page. Alternatively, see the method of embedding Flash in the adding Flash to pages manually technique.

Ajax

388 Ajax: cool effects

Ajax is best known for creating cool effects on the page. For example, visit www.rapha.cc and add something to your shopping cart. You'll notice that the page doesn't have to reload, and the small cart simply appears with a nice little flash of color that slowly fades away.

389 Ajax: what is it?

Ajax is the term used to describe a set of methods for creating "rich" desktop-like applications on the web. It allows applications to side-step the traditional "request information > refresh browser" model used on the web, making for a more seamless user experience.

390 Ajax: what does it stand for?

Although originally intended as an acronym (for Asynchronus JavaScript and XML) it soon became clear that it didn't really hold true: XML is not a requirement of Ajax applications. The person who coined the term Ajax, Jesse James Garrett, updated his original essay to make it clear that Ajax (or AJAX as it first appeared) is not an acronym.

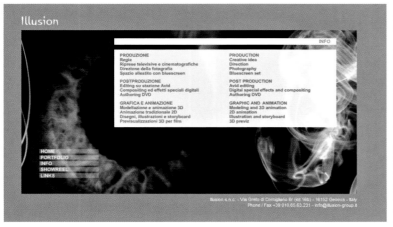

391 Ajax: where to begin

Ajax requires knowledge of several technologies; some of which are fairly straightforward. For example, you will need to know about standards-compliant HTML and CSS. But it's JavaScript and DOM Scripting that make Ajax tick, and these are rather more advanced. If you feel you are experienced enough with HTML/CSS and ready to move on, then Jeremy Keith's book *Bulletproof Ajax* is an excellent place to start.

392 Ajax: technologies

Ajax is not itself a "technology," rather, it makes use of technologies that have existed for years on the web, including HTML/XHTML, CSS, JavaScript, DOM Scripting, and XMLHttpRequest.

393 Ajax: using Dreamweaver's tools

Dreamweaver CS3 includes new tools for creating Ajax applications. You will still need a good understanding of the underlying principles, but it will allow you to get started with Ajax while removing some of the pain of learning JavaScript.

394 Ajax: what about my "back" button?

There is a potential problem with Ajax, in that web users are used to pressing the "back" button to return to a previous page. With an Ajax application, however, you tend not to go from page to page as the data is loaded into the current page. This effectively disables the "back" button. In the future, this might not be such a problem; users will learn the new behavior, and browsers are likely to adapt to the new methods too.

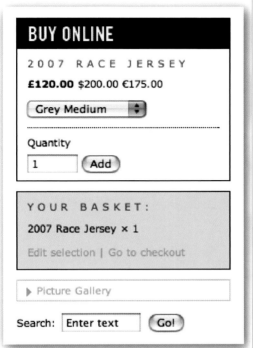

395 Ajax: where to see it in action

Examples of Ajax in use can be seen on the following websites:
- www.bulletproofajax.com
- www.clearnova.com/ajax/

396 Ajax: alternatives

So, you want a rich interface that doesn't require the browser to reload every time you interact with the page? Sounds a lot like Flash! If you don't fancy taking the plunge with JavaScript, you might find that building simple Flash applications gives you the functionality you need along with high-quality animations.

397 Animated rollovers

Rollover buttons tend to use GIF images for the over and off states, but there's no reason why the GIFs have to be static. One or both of the images could be animated, leading to some very neat effects.

Background images

398 Background images in menus: step 1

Work through the CSS Rollover Menu and Horizontal rollover menu techniques as essential background to this series of techniques. The benefit of using images (as opposed to simple background colors) is that you can create more complex, polished designs. This technique still uses HTML text for the wording, so it retains many advantages of the other techniques too. Start by duplicating the HTML and CSS files created in Horizontal rollover menu and giving them suitable names.

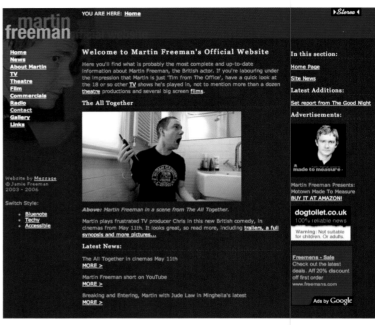

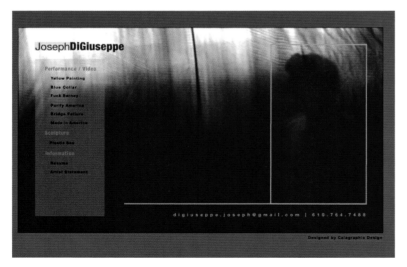

399 Background images in menus: step 2

Create a pair of JPEG images, one for the "normal" state (in blue); the other will be for the "rollover" (in green). The images should be 100 pixels high and about 10 pixels wide. They should fade from light to dark, reaching the darkest color about 30 pixels from the top. We will only see the top 30 pixels of the image; the rest is there as a safety net in case the user has resized their text for personal preference.

400 Background images in menus: step 3

There are no changes to make to the HTML—you're still using a simple unordered list. All the editing takes place in the CSS. In the "head a" style replace the **background-color: #9FF;** line to read **background: URL(images/menu_blue.jpg);** Similarly, in "head a:hover," change **background-color: #9F0;** to read **background: URL(images/menu_green.jpg);**

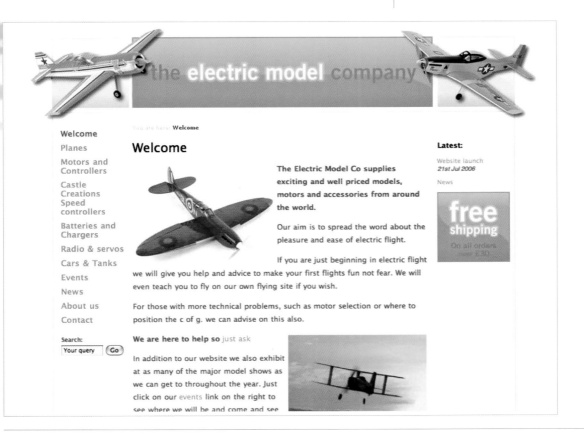

401 Background images in menus: step 4

Now we're going to add an extra bit of styling, just for fun. In the "head a:hover" style add **color: #FF0;** to turn the text yellow on rollover. And to give it a nice thick underline for added effect put this in too:

border-bottom: 4px solid #FF0;

CSS rollover menus

402 CSS rollover menu

Combine this approach with one of the multicolumn CSS layout techniques (see tips 208-213) to create a neat left-hand menu. It will be accessible and standards-compliant because it simply uses an unordered list for the menu, and CSS to style it and create the rollover effect. This version uses no images, which makes it very simple and quick to implement.

403 CSS rollover menu: step 1

Assuming you have already set up a multicolumn page, you need to add an unordered list into the "col1" div. See tips 266-269 for details, putting each menu item into its own **<li>** tag, e.g. **<li>About me</li> <li>My Pictures</li>** etc.

404 CSS rollover menu: step 2

Now make each of your items into a list by adding **<a>** tags around them, within the **<li>** tags. Each one should look like this:

<li><a href="about_me.htm">About me</a></li>

405 CSS rollover menu: step 3

That's it for the HTML! One of the best aspects of this technique is it requires very little code. Now the fun starts and we can style the list. We need to make sure this styling only applies to the menu list, not all lists. We can target the menu list because it is within the "col1" div by adding the following to the stylesheet: **#col1 ul{ }**

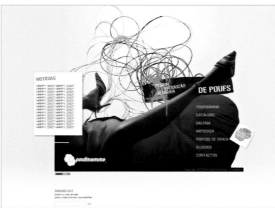

406 CSS rollover menu: step 4

Any attributes that relate specifically to the menu list can now be added within those curly brackets. The first thing we want to do is get rid of the default bullet points, so add this line within the curly brackets: **list-style: none;**

407 CSS rollover menu: step 5

The bullet points should now have disappeared, but the menu will still be indented from the side of the page. Add **display: inline;** to fix that.

408 CSS rollover menu: step 6

Now we'll create some styles specifically for the links within the menu. That means these styles will target **<a>** tags within the "col1" div, which we do by adding a line like this to the stylesheet: **#col1 a { }**. We can add our styles within the brackets as before. Start with a background color: **background-color: #9FF;** then test the page in your browser.

409 CSS rollover menu: step 7

You should see some links with a background color that only extends to the width of each link. Let's fix that first by adding **display: block;** to the style. We can also separate each of the menu items by putting a thin space between them, like this: **margin-bottom: 1px;** and it will now start to look much more like a menu.

410 CSS rollover menu: step 8

You can give each of your menu items a little more room around the text by giving them "padding," like this: **padding: 5px;** (Change the 5 to a higher number for more space, or a lower number for less space.)

411 CSS rollover menu: step 9

Finally, we get to the "rollover" part of the technique! Create a new line in your stylesheet like this: **#col1 a:hover { }** and we'll add the appropriate styles within those brackets again. (Note that these will only apply to links within the "col1" div.)

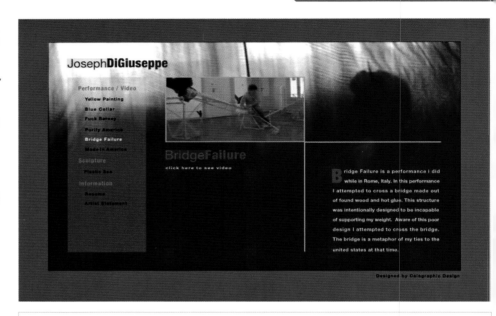

412 CSS rollover menu: step 10

Our rollover behavior is going to be fairly simple: the background and text color will change, highlighting the chosen item. Add **background-color: #9F0;** into the line we just made, followed by **color: #090;**

413 CSS rollover menu: summary

You should now have a menu that's as wide as your left-hand column, with dark blue text on a light blue background. The menu items should change to dark green on a light green background as you mouse over them. You will notice that if you have a menu item that's long enough to require two lines, this technique accommodates that by simply making the blue panel higher.

414 Displaying today's date

It's an old trick but still one with some value; displaying the current date at the top of the page can help give the impression that the site is frequently maintained. (Of course, the best way to do this is to frequently update the content!) The next couple of techniques show how to do this using different technologies.

415 Checking for PHP

Checking whether your server has PHP installed is very simple. Create a page called info.php and type in the following:

```
<?php phpinfo(); ?>
```

Upload to your server and display it in your browser. If you see the same text then PHP is not running. Otherwise you should see all the current parameters related to PHP as well as lots of other useful server information.

416 Displaying today's date with PHP: 1

Make sure your server is running PHP and that your page uses the .php suffix. Add this code where you want the date to appear:

```
<?php print  date("l dS of F Y"); ?>
```

Load your page in a browser and you should see the date displayed like this: "Sunday 27th of May 2008."

417 Displaying today's date with PHP: 2

To display the date in different formats you can change the values within the brackets of the previous example. Try these out to learn how the values affect the display:

("m-d-y") displays as "05-27-07"
("m-d-Y") displays as "05-27-2007"
("Y:m:d") displays as "2007:05:27"
("dS of F") displays as "2007:05:27"

418 Displaying today's date with PHP: 3

Put your date script into its own .php file and simply "include" it into all the pages on your site. Then if you wish to update it (e.g. change the way the date is formatted) you only need to edit one file. Your script should contain only the single line of PHP code from the previous examples. Save it as "date.php" and add this code to the pages you want the date to appear on:

```
<?php include("date.php"); ?>
```

Google AdSense

419 Earning money from Google AdSense

A great way to earn income from your website is by placing advertising on it and Google AdSense makes this process really easy. You're not likely to get rich quick this way unless your website has very heavy traffic, but the occasional check for $100 from Google is welcome nonetheless. The following entries take you through this comparatively simple process.

420 Google AdSense: step 1

First you need to understand what AdSense is. Google reads the text of your pages looking for keywords, finds adverts that match these keywords, then displays them on your site. People only see ads that are relevant to the subject of the web page they are looking at, which means they're less likely to be annoyed by irrelevant adverts, and are more likely to click through to the advertiser's site. Each click earns you money (paid for by the advertiser) which Google pays when a threshold is reached.

421 Google AdSense: step 2

Start the process by visiting www.google.com/adsense to sign up for the service. Enter the address of the site, plus your name and address. Be careful to do this accurately because Google will send your money by check to that address, made out to that name.

422 Google AdSense: step 3

You will receive an email from Google letting you know that your submission has been successful. Follow the instructions to confirm your application, and you will then be able to log in to your AdSense account.

423 Google AdSense: step 4

Once you've logged in, click the AdSense Setup palette, and then the AdSense for Content link. On the subsequent page, select the default "Ad unit" and stick with text-only ads for now. They are my preference as they are not too distracting from the rest of a site. Also, you can control the look and feel to some extent, which is not possible with image-based ads.

426 Google AdSense: step 7

This final page displays the code you will need to paste into your website wherever you want the ads to appear. This is actually a simple JavaScript, and you shouldn't edit it unless you are sure of what you are doing. Having said that, read on to find out about editing the JavaScript!

427 Google AdSense: step 8

The JavaScript contains basic HTML color references in the "hexadecimal" format, and these can be easily edited. That means you could, for example, change the background color of your ads without having to go back through the Google AdSense setup pages.

428 Google AdSense: step 9

Pasting the advert into dozens of pages on your site is all well and good, unless you decide you want to change a color or the format. Much better is to use an "include" technique (see tips 195-196), meaning you only have to update one copy of the ad to have the effects instantly updated across your entire site.

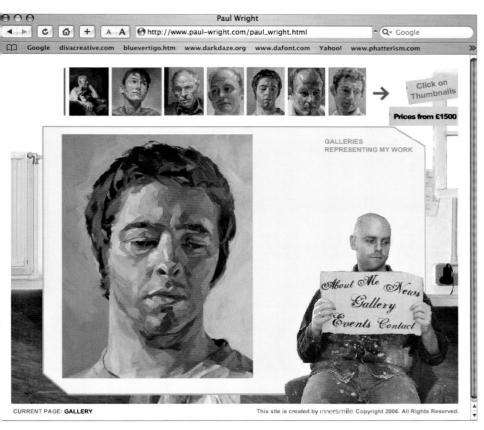

424 Google AdSense: step 5

This page allows you to specify the format (i.e. size and shape) of the ad, as well as the colors. Choose the size which best matches that available on your site, and use the built-in color selector to pick an appropriate color scheme. Bear in mind that if you choose colors that match your site too closely the ads might not stand out enough to be effective.

425 Google AdSense: step 6

The "channels" page is next, but it won't mean much to you for now as you have no channels set up. Channels allow you to get more detailed reports on how specific pages or ads are performing. For now though you should ignore this page and click through to the next one.

Fireworks rollover menus

429 Fireworks rollover menu

Fireworks allows you to create a menu with a simple rollover effect really easily. This isn't my preferred method (see the tips on CSS image replacement and CSS rollover menu for a best-practice approach) but it will get you up and running quickly.

430 Fireworks rollover menu 1: visual design

Start by creating a visual design of how you'd like your menu to appear. Each menu item should be of similar appearance to make it clear to users that it is a menu. If you place it in the top left of the screen it will further help users know what to expect. Keep each item big enough that it will be easy to click on.

431 Fireworks rollover menu 2: the rollover state

Now duplicate the first frame so that your document has two identical frames, and select the second frame. Change something about the appearance of the menu, for example the background color, or give the text a highlighting glow. The only limitation is that the overall dimensions of each menu item must remain the same.

432 Fireworks rollover menu 3: slice and dice

Now select the Slice tool and draw slice areas around each menu item. It usually creates a smoother result for the user if you make the menu areas butt up against each other. You can name each slice if you prefer, but Fireworks will automatically do the job for you.

433 Fireworks rollover menu 4: adding the links

Each menu item obviously needs to link to a page within your site. For example, if the top item is called "Home" you would want it to link to index.htm or similar. Click on each slice in turn and in the properties tab simply enter the url. (It's easy isn't it? You don't even have to create an HTML link!)

434 Fireworks rollover menu 5: adding the behavior

Select all of the slices and click on the little target icon on one of the slices. In the menu that appears select "Add Simple Rollover Behavior." Behind the scenes, Fireworks has kindly prepared a JavaScript for you.

435 Fireworks rollover menu 6: outputting the HTML

All that remains is to output the HTML. Select Export from the Edit menu and ensure that "HTML and Images" is selected in the Save As drop-down. Also make sure that "Current Frame Only" is not selected. Choose the location you want to save the files to, click Save, and you're done!

436 Fireworks rollover menu 7: testing your menu

Open the resulting HTML file in your browser, and check the menu is working as you envisaged. Move your mouse over the menu items and you should see whichever highlight effect you designed. You should also go to the correct HTML page when you click each item. If there are any errors, simply go back to your Fireworks document, tweak it, and export it again.

437 Flash animation basics

Creating animations in Flash is really straightforward. This set of tips creates a simple but effective animation that demonstrates some of the basic Flash animation techniques.

438 Highlighting techniques

There are a number of ways in which you can indicate that an area (e.g. a button, an image) is a link when the user moves their mouse over it. You can add a glow, a shadow, change the color, or any number of different visual effects. The following tips and techniques describe some effective methods.

439 Highlighting technique 1: glow

Adding a glow to a link makes it look like the area is "turned on" when the user mouses over it. This is particularly effective on text on a dark-colored background. In some programs you can do this by simply selecting the "glow" effect. A more manual approach is to duplicate the layer with the text and apply a gaussian blur filter. Making the text lighter (e.g. from light gray to white) enhances the effect.

440 Highlighting technique 2: drop shadow

The drop-shadow technique is easy to apply, but can be highly effective. It has the effect of "lifting" the item off the page, making it appear three-dimensional. It works well on text, but can happily apply to buttons and other shapes too. Most graphics programs have a drop-shadow function, but make sure you tweak the settings to get the effect you want, not the one the software wants!

Horizontal rollover menus

441 Horizontal rollover menu: step 1

The next tips are for creating a horizontal version of the CSS rollover menu, using the same essential ingredients, so you'll need to go through those first. You should also review the steps in the header and footer layout technique (see tips 259–264) as they are applied here also. Start by duplicating the page created in CSS rollover menu and give it a suitable name.

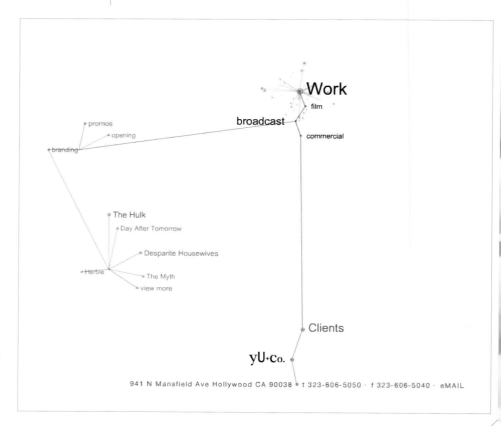

442 Horizontal rollover menu: step 2

In the HTML, edit the name of the "col1" div to read "head," like this: **<div id="head">** You should ensure that this div is right at the top of your page, just after the opening **<body>** tag, as we want our menu to be right at the top in this example.

443 Horizontal rollover menu: step 3

You'll see that the styles no longer work; that's because your menu is now within a div called "head" and the styles refer to a div called "col1". Edit all instances of "col1" in your stylesheet to read "head," and in the HTML change **<div id="col1">** to read **<div id="head">**

444 Horizontal rollover menu: step 4

The following style, added to your stylesheet, will make the "head" div expand to the entire width of the page: **#head { width: 100%; }** (see the header and footer layout techniques for details).

445 Horizontal rollover menu: step 5

We no longer need space below each item, so the line **margin-bottom: 1px;** must be changed to **margin-right: 1px;** to control the space between each item horizontally. The number can be changed higher or lower to add more or less space, and can even be negative (e.g. "-3px") if needs be.

446 Horizontal rollover menu: step 6

Remove the line **display: block;** from the "head a" style and add a whole new style, like this: **#head li { display: inline; }** Refresh the page and you'll see that the menu is now horizontal, and that each item expands to take up only the amount of space it needs.

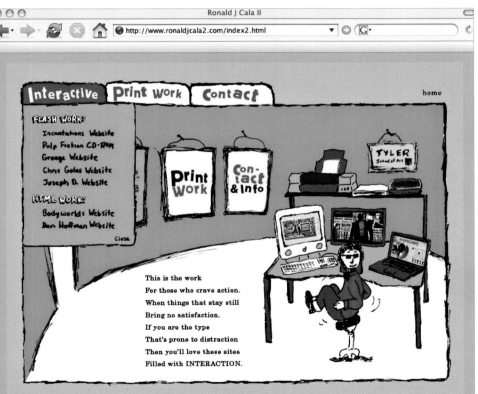

Password protection

447 Password protecting a directory

If you have sensitive information on your website you can take steps to stop unauthorized users from accessing it. Typically this will require the user to input a username and password; if they get either wrong they will not be able to see the content. The following work-through shows how to password protect a directory (and its contents) on the most popular web server, Apache.

448 Password protecting a directory: step 1

We'll be using a technique referred to as "htaccess." The result is that everything placed in the specific directory (folder) is protected automatically, including subdirectories, so you don't have to worry about individual files. You will need two files: .htaccess will go in the directory you want to protect, and .htpasswd will go elsewhere on your server.

449 Password protecting a directory: step 2

There are a number of online password generators, which are probably the most convenient way of carrying out this step. Do a web search for "htpasswd generator" and simply enter the username and password you wish to use. The generator will return a line of text containing your username followed by a colon and an encrypted version of your password. It will look something like this:

jamie:amaIUcbRIj3VY

450 Password protecting a directory: step 3

Paste the line of text into a plain text file, name it "htpasswd" and copy it to your server, ideally into an area such as your cgi-bin, or the directory above your "web" or "public_html" directory. This will prevent people from seeing the file. Once it's in place, rename the file, adding a period at the start, like this: .htpasswd

451 Password protecting a directory: step 4

Create a file called "htaccess" and add in the following text:

```
AuthName "My Folder"
AuthType Basic
AuthUserFile /www/mysite.com/.htpasswd
Require valid-user
<Limit GET POST> require valid-user </Limit>
```

452 Password protecting a directory: step 5

"My Folder" is text that will appear in the log-in window, so change that to something appropriate. The AuthUserFile value is more critical, requiring a "full path" to your .htaccess file. Your server may be set up differently. Another path pattern might be **/home/my_username/.htpasswd** for example, but you may need to contact your ISP to find the correct path for you.

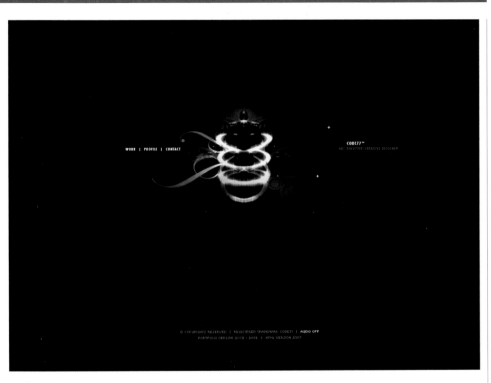

453 Password protecting a directory: step 6

When you try to access the directory—or any content within the directory—you will now be shown a password prompt. Enter the username and password you set in step 2 and you will be allowed to see it. You won't have to enter the password again until you quit your browser.

454 Password protecting a directory: step 7

You can add more username/password combinations to the .htpasswd file to allow many users access. This is more secure than simply giving everyone the same password as it means you could, if needed, bar one particular user simply by deleting their line from the file.

455 Password protection with control panels

Many hosting packages provide a "control panel" allowing you to carry out complex server configuration through a simple interface. A common example is password protecting certain areas of your site. This can be done manually, but why not take the easy option?

456 Generating an .htpasswd file: step 1

If you have "command line" access to your server (e.g. SSH or Telnet) you should be able to create a password file manually. At the command prompt, navigate to the location you want to create the password file.

457 Generating an .htpasswd file: step 2

Type this text: **htpasswd -c .htpasswd jamie** and hit the return key. You will be asked to enter the password you want to use, and then to confirm it. Each time, type it in carefully and hit return. Your new password file will now exist in the location you specified.

458 Generating an .htpasswd file: step 3

Let's briefly examine that command so you understand what you just did. Firstly, **htpasswd** tells the server which "program" to run. **-c** tells htpasswd to create a new file (c stands for "create"), called ".htpasswd." Note the dot at the start of the filename; this hides it from anyone without the "permission" to see it.

459 Generating an .htpasswd file: step 4

This password won't do anything without a corresponding ".htaccess" file referring to it; see tip 451 for details. If you want more user-name/password combinations you can add them to the file you just made, rather than create a new file each time. We'll do that next.

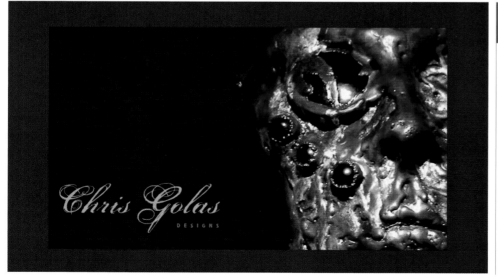

460 Generating an .htpasswd file: step 5

Type a similar command at the prompt, like so: **htpasswd .htpasswd bob** then enter Bob's password, and confirm it. Eagle-eyed readers will see that we simply left out the command to create (**-c**) a new file, but put in the name of the existing one. You can add as many users as you like in this way, but if the number becomes too great it can start to get hard to manage.

Image protection

461 Preventing image theft

To embed an image on a page, all you need is the image URL, whether it's on your domain or another one entirely. There may be times when you don't want people to use your content in this way. For example, a particularly popular image could cost you dearly in terms of bandwidth.

462 Preventing image theft: step 1

Firstly, decide which content you want to restrict in this way, and place it all in the same directory. You could simply choose to protect everything in the images/directory, or even the entire site. Create a blank text file in the location you choose.

463 Preventing image theft: step 2

Type the following into the file and save it:

```
RewriteEngine on
RewriteCond %{HTTP_REFERER} !^$
RewriteCond %{HTTP_REFERER} !^http://www.your_site.com/.*$
[NC]
ReWriteRule .*\.(gif|jpg)$ - [N,F,L]
```

The first line invokes an Apache module which "rewrites" certain HTTP requests (e.g. an image request from a web page) according to the "conditions" set in the next line. This basically says "no requests from any other domain is allowed." The third line says "except this one!" which is typically your own site. The last line defines the file types that are affected by the rule; in this case GIF and JPEGs, but you could also include PDFs, MP3s, etc.

464 Preventing image theft: step 3

If you wish to allow certain third-party sites to embed your content (for example, partner sites or reviewers) you can just add another line like that shown in line three. Simply put their domain name in place of yours..

465 Preventing image theft: step 4

When you've carried out these steps you need to check carefully that it's working as expected. This technique is very powerful and if you make an error in the code you could suddenly find yourself without any images on your website! If that happens, remove the .htaccess file and examine the code; you'll probably find you've simply mistyped something.

466 Preventing image theft: step 5

Finally, a note on this technique. I take copyright of my content very seriously, but at the same time I generally prefer to send a polite email to someone "stealing" my content to ask them to link back to my site. That way, they get to use my content, but I get the benefit of third-party links (which is great for search engine optimization) and increased traffic. Think very carefully before you decide to lock your content down.

467 Watermark your images

A simple way to protect your images is to watermark them with the URL of your site. Even if people do use them on their sites you at least get the benefit of publicity for your own site, and hopefully a few extra visitors. Don't let the watermark totally obscure the image though!

Hacking

468 Protection from hacking

Your hosting provider should have set up your server with a certain amount of security built-in. However, there's much you can do yourself to ensure your site stays unmolested. The following tips aim to tell you a little about the way malicious hackers work, and some ways of protecting your site–and your visitors.

469 Protection from hacking: 1

Use strong passwords. If you have a password protected area there's no point having a username of "admin" and a password of "password" or the most casual attempt at unauthorized entry will succeed.

470 Protection from hacking: 2

Hackers employ a technique known as "dictionary attack." They repeatedly try username and password combinations by running through hundreds of thousands of common words, phrases, numbers, and combinations until they get lucky. That's why you should always use random strings of characters for passwords, not just "jamie123" for example.

471 Protection from hacking: 3

Hackers are experts at programming computers to plough through huge amounts of data very quickly. That's the reason longer passwords are more secure; the number of possible combinations goes up exponentially with every extra character.

472 Protection from hacking: 4

Hacking techniques are used to "harvest" email addresses, which are then used by spammers and other hackers. If you are capturing email data on your website, make sure it's stored in a secure format, such as a MySQL database. If your script simply writes data to a text file called "users.txt" it won't be long before someone sniffs it out.

473 Protection from hacking: 5

If your web hosting provider hasn't already done so, you should check that all the latest security patches are installed, and that no "ports" are left open if they are not needed. (Ports are designated to specific services, such as email, FTP, SSH, etc.)

474 Protection from hacking: 6

It can be dangerous to install third-party scripts and programs on your website unless you understand what they are actually doing. Even if you don't fully understand the programming, you can read through the code and look for tell-tale signs such as references to third-party URLs.

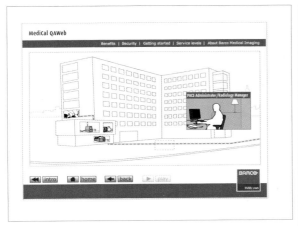

475 Protection from hacking: 7

If you have user-updateable pages—a forum perhaps, or blog comments—it would be easy for someone to insert HTML code that causes trouble. For example, they could simply load images that cause offence. You need to "validate" the form input before it's accepted, to strip out all but the most basic HTML tags, for example.

476 Quick and dirty password protection

Less secure and less flexible than using htaccess is the technique of "obfuscation." Hide a directory from most eyes simply by giving it an unusual, unguessable name, such as jUsd39~21. This is effectively like using a password but no username, which immediately makes it half as secure as "proper" methods. However, it can be extremely handy if you have no other options.

Flash portfolios

477 Simple Flash portfolio

Flash is great for making simple applications that look good with rich interactivity. In this next walk-through we're going to create a Flash portfolio that fades to white between each image, giving a smooth, professional feel. Each image will have a white border, giving a "photo print" effect.

478 Simple Flash portfolio: step 1

Open the Flash application and set up a new document that's 640-480 pixels in size. Select a mid-gray for the background color to offset the white photo border. Create five Layers in your Timeline, called Actions, Frame, Images, Fader, and Controls, then save the document.

479 Simple Flash portfolio: step 2

Select the "Frame" layer and draw a centered white rectangle 500 pixels by 380 pixels, without an outline. Select the rectangle and hit F8 to turn it into a Movie Clip, named "Rectangle."

480 Simple Flash portfolio: step 3

In your preferred image editor (e.g. Photoshop, Fireworks, etc.) prepare six images by scaling them to 480-360 pixels, and saving them as high-quality JPEGs. Flash will compress them again, so you need to start with good quality files. Import them into Flash using the "Import to Library" command. Open up the Library window (F11) and you should get six icons representing your images.

481 Simple Flash portfolio: step 4

Click on frame 11 in the Timeline, in the Images Layer, and press Shift-F5 to add a keyframe. Do the same on frame 21, 31, 41, 51, and 71. Open the Library tab and drag image 1 into frame 11, image 2 into frame 22, and so on. Make sure the images are centered.

482 Simple Flash portfolio: step 5

Create a new blank Movie Clip called "Fade." Drag the Rectangle movie from the Library onto the main window and center it. Add keyframes at frames 5 and 9. Go to frame 1, select the rectangle and change its Alpha value to 0 percent to make it transparent. Do the same at frame 9. Add a tween style of "Motion" to frames 1 and 5.

483 Simple Flash portfolio: step 6

In the "Photoframe" layer select frame 71 and press F5 to add a frame. This has the effect of making the Rectangle appear on all frames in the movie, so it will always appear behind your images. If you play the movie at this stage you should see the images appearing in order. Now we'll add the fade effect...

484 Simple Flash portfolio: step 7

Now, go back to the main timeline, put a keyframe at frame 6 on the "Fader" Layer and drag the Fader movie from the Library and center it carefully. Duplicate this keyframe to frame 16, 26, 36, 46, 56, and 66, then add blank keyframes at frames 15, 25, 35, 45, 55, and 65. In the Control menu, select Test Movie to see your work so far. You should see the images appearing between white fades. Now we need to add some controls...

485 Simple Flash portfolio: step 8

Select frame one of the "Actions" Layer and open the ActionScript editor in "Expert" mode (trust me!). Type in a **stop();** command. This will stop the movie from playing until the user tells it to play. Duplicate this keyframe onto frames 11, 21, 31, 41, 51, 61, and 71.

486 Simple Flash portfolio: step 9

Flash has some nice-looking buttons built-in, so pick a play button, or design your own. You also need a rewind button, which will allow your users to return to the beginning of the portfolio. On frame one of the "Controls" Layer, place the play button at the bottom right of the screen, and the rewind button at the bottom left. Select the play button and open the ActionScript editor.

487 Simple Flash portfolio: step 10

The movie currently stops every 10 frames. The play button will override this command, so the user can continue on to the next image once they're ready. Type in **on (release) { play(); }** then select the rewind button and type **on (release) { gotoAndStop(1); }** into the ActionScript window. Test your movie to try out the controls.

488 Simple Flash portfolio: step 11

Now all that's left is to add some text to the first and last frames of the portfolio; welcoming users at the start, and thanking them at the end. On frame one in the "Images" Layer type in some appropriate text, and do the same on frame 71. Test your movie, and you're done! See the tips on adding Flash (see tips 377-383) to your pages to get your portfolio into your website.

PHP portfolios

489 Simple PHP portfolio

In this series of tips, we'll create a portfolio that's really easy to update. Your server will need to be set up to run the PHP scripting language, and you'll have to make the page look pretty using CSS techniques. Start by making sure PHP is running on your server.

490 Simple PHP portfolio: step 1

Start by preparing your images. You'll need thumbnails 100 pixels wide, and full-size images 320 pixels wide. Name all the thumbnails thumb_pic_0.jpg, thumb_pic_1.jpg, and so on. The main images should be named pic_0.jpg, pic_1.jpg, etc. Put all the images in a directory called Folder within another called Portfolio.

491 Simple PHP portfolio: step 2

Create a basic two column layout page named "portfolio.php" (see tips 208-210) and in the left-hand column place an include to pull in the thumbnails images. Type this text:

```php
<?php include("thumbnails.php");?>
```

492 Simple PHP portfolio: step 3

The thumbnails.php page is the trickiest part of this technique, but it only involves a few lines of code. We start by entering the number of images you have in your portfolio. In this case we have five images, so type this on a new line after your opening PHP tag:

```php
$total = 5;
$i = 0;
```

493 Simple PHP portfolio: step 4

Next we'll add a "do/while" statement, meaning PHP will run the script (do) while a certain condition is true; in this case, that the number of pictures is not higher than the maximum we just specified. Put a return in, then type:

```php
do {
} while ($i < $total);
```

494 Simple PHP portfolio: step 5

In between the curly brackets of the "do/while" statement, add this code:

```php
echo "<a href=\"index.php?image=$i=\">";
echo "<img src=\"images/thumb_pic_$i.jpg\"></a> ";
$i ++;
```

That last line increments the counter (@$i@) so that the next time the script loops round it will display a picture with a higher number—which is why you numbered the images!

About Me News
Gallery
Events Contact

CLICK HERE TO VIEW MY CV

About Me

After training as an Illustrator, I have spent the last decade developing a painterly language through which I seek to capture a vitality beyond the establishment of a mere 'likeness' to the subject.

Whilst I appreciate the importance of the individual being recognisable, the subjects are glimpsed rather than exposed, their inner selves hinted at but ultimately inscrutable.

Though I often work on a large, potentially imposing scale, the work remains approachable

495 Simple PHP portfolio: step 6

Test the index page in your browser and you should see five small images down the left-hand side. Rolling over the images will reveal that they are links, but as yet clicking on them will have no effect; first you need to create a new PHP page named "images.php" and include it in the second column **<div>** as before.

496 Simple PHP portfolio: step 7

The portfolio relies on a variable called "image" being passed in the URL. That's why the links from the thumbnail images have ?image=X added to the end. Our new page will use that number to decide which image to show. Type this line of code after the opening PHP tag in images.php:

```
echo "<img src=\"images/pic_$image.jpg\">";
```

497 Simple PHP portfolio: step 8

Test in your browser, and you'll see a missing image icon in the right column. Click on one of the thumbnail links and the main image will magically appear, because you've now passed the "image" variable in the URL. You can remedy this by adding the following before the previous "echo" command:

```
if ($_GET["image"] == NULL){
$_GET["images"] = 0;
} $image = $_GET["images"];
```

498 Simple PHP portfolio: step 9

The previous step gave the script a default value for the "image" variable in case none was found in the URL, as would be the case when the user first arrived at the portfolio. An even simpler (although less robust) way of dealing with that would be to include the image variable in the link to your portfolio, for example:

```
<a href="portfolio/index.php?image=0">My Portfolio</a>
```

499 Simple PHP portfolio: step 10

The simple portfolio is now complete. However, it is not very accessible—there's no alt text on the images, nor are there any headings or captions. The sequence does show you some good basic PHP though, and other tips in this book will allow you to embellish the basic script.

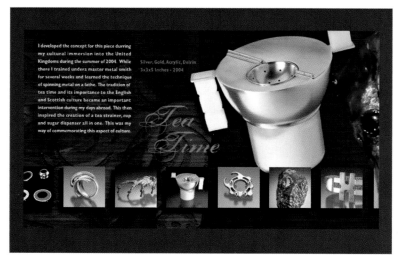

500 Remember the user

No matter how interesting and cool you make your user interface always remember the poor user! They are, after all, the point of your labors, and without them your website would be meaningless.

Featured designers

2FRESH
www.2fresh.com

Artiva Design
www.artiva.it

Michael Browers
www.michaelbrowers.com

Ronald J. Cala
www.ronaldjcala2.com

Clearleft
www.clearleft.com

Code 77
www.code77.com

Dpi Vision
www.dpivision.com

Antonin Ferla
www.antoninferla.com

Futurelab
www.futurelab.org.uk

FXstyle
www.fxstyle.com

GriGri
www.grigri.be

Joe Holdcroft
www.joeholdcroft.com

Hostblue
www.hostblue.co.uk

Rick Huby
www.batleyanddewsbury.co.uk

Innersmile
www.innersmile.biz

Inol3
www.inol3.com

Martin Ivanov
www.acidmartin.wemakesites.net

Colin Jenkinson
www.icons.org.uk

Anthony Johnston
www.cv.antix.co.uk

Jorge Jorge
www.jorgejorge.com

Patrick H. Lauke
www.salford.ac.uk

Gustavo Machado
www.gustavo-machado.com

Mayhem Studios
www.mayhemstudios.com

Laura McCarthy
www.kermitspad.piczo.com

Richard McCoy
www.mccoy.co.uk

Message
www.message.uk.com

Mojo Studios
www.mojostudios.com

MusaWorkLab
www.musaworklab.com

NG Design
www.ngdesign.it

Pure Imagination Studio
www.pureimaginationstudio.com

Rareport
www.rareport.com

Raspberry Frog
www.raspberryfrog.co.uk

Rehybrid
www.rehybrid.com

Ben Scott
www.ben-scott.co.uk

Grace Smith
www.postscript5.co.uk

Tim Smith
www.mypoorbrain.com

Steilvorlage
www.steilvorlage.de

Chris Taylor
www.stillbreathing.co.uk

Howard Taylor
www.cancho.co.uk

Trait
www.traitstudio.com

Arslan Volkan
www.hillside.com.tr

Simon Wiffen
www.simonwiffen.co.uk

Work in Progress Design
www.workinprogressdesign.co.uk

yU+co
www.yuco.com

Glossary

Accessibility

Also known as "web accessibility," this means making sure that your site can be used by the widest group of people possible, regardless of physical or cognitive ability.

Ajax

A series of techniques used to create desktop-like applications on the web, avoiding the page refresh normally associated with web browsing.

Alt text

Within the "image" tag the alt text describes the content of the image for users who can't see it. This is a basic accessibility technique, as well as being helpful in SEO.

Apache

Open-source web server software that typically runs on Unix-based operating systems such as Linux.

Browser

Software used to display and interact with websites. Examples include Internet Explorer, Safari, and Firefox.

Cache

An area of memory set aside to store pages and objects (e.g. images) from web pages from your web browsing history.

Client-side

Software that runs on a user's own computer, rather than on the server, for example JavaScript. (This means that if JavaScript is not installed on the user's computer, the application will fail.)

Cross-platform

A "platform" is essentially the operating system, such as Windows or Mac OS. "Cross-platform" refers to making websites operate correctly regardless of the system being used.

CSS

Short for Cascading Style Sheets, this technology is used to control the styling of web pages. CSS is a W3C standard.

Dynamic

This refers to web pages created on-the-fly, usually with information drawn from a database or from user input. This allows the user experience to be highly customized and up-to-date.

Flash

Software for creating rich-media applications (e.g. animations, videos, games) on the web. Requires the Flash plug-in to run the resulting "SWF" files.

GIF

An image format best suited to graphical images with few graduations and a small color range.

Hacking

Usually refers to the activities of criminal software programmers, but it really means any programming of software code. Programmers often refer to themselves as "hackers."

HTAccess

Part of the Apache web server software that controls aspects of configuration such as how to process certain page types, or limiting access to a directory.

HTML

Hypertext Markup Language is used to create web pages. The code defines the structure and content of a web page by using various tags added to the text.

Image compression

There are several ways of reducing the file size of an image, usually with an associated drop in quality. Examples include JPEG and GIF.

Information architecture (IA)

For our purposes, IA relates to the organization of the content and functions of a website in a logical manner.

Java

Java is a server-side prgramming language only really used for larger-scale web applications. Has nothing to do with Java-Script.

JavaScript

A scripting language widely used in web pages and applications. JavaScript is a client-side language. It is totally unrelated to Java.

JPEG

An image format that is good for full-color images such as photographs. Can be compressed to different degrees of quality.

Keywords

Those words most associated with the content in question. These are the words likely to be used by search engine users to find your site.

LAMP

This acronym stands for Linux, Apache, MySQL, and PHP, and is used as a short-hand way of describing a particular open-source web server "environment."

Link

The very foundation of the web, links are clickable objects (usually text or images) that take the user from one URL to another. They can also trigger an action such as running a script. Also known as "hyperlinks."

Lists

There are several types of list in HTML, the most common being unordered (<ul>) and ordered (<ol>). The former appear with bullet points, the latter with numbers.

Menu

A collection of links that lead to the main areas or important content of a website. The menu usually also reflects the structure of the site.

MySQL

Database language often used in conjunction with Apache and PHP. MySQL is an open-source alternative to commercial software such as Microsoft SQL.

Navigation

Sometimes used as a noun interchangeably with "menu," this word is also a verb, decribing the act of moving from place to place within a site.

Open source

Software where the source code is open to use and development by all, so long as those modifications are offered back to the community under the same terms. Often, but not always, free to the end user. Examples include Linux, Apache, MySql, and PHP.

PHP

PHP is a powerful but easy to learn open-source scripting language, often associated with Apache and MySQL. PHP is a "server-side" language.

Script

A set of instructions carried out by another program (e.g. PHP or JavaScript). Can be written as a stand-alone code document, or embedded within an HTML or other web page.

Search engine

Software service allowing you to search the web. Some use "crawlers" to create a database (e.g. Google) while directories (e.g. Yahoo!) use human editors.

Semantic markup

Using tags that appropriately describe the meaning of the content. For example, a main heading would be marked up as <h1> rather than simply as "large, bold text."

SEO

Acronym for Search Engine Optimization, the act of making your website content perform as well as possible in search engine rankings.

Server-side

Software that runs on the server rather than on the user's own computer. For example, PHP.

Table

A series of rows and columns used to structure tabular data. In web pages this is achieved using the <table>, <tr>, and <td> tags.

Tag

Tags are a way of "marking up" text in order that a browser or other software can render it in some way. For example, to turn some text into a headline or paragraph.

URL

This stands for "Uniform Resource Locator," and is the unique address of every single object of the internet; no two items can share the same URL.

Usability

The art and science of making websites "usable" by designing them around the users' goals and requirements, rather than the designer's personal preferences.

W3C

The World Wide Web Consortium is an international group of organizations involved with the World Wide Web. Founded by Tim Berners-Lee; architect of the web.

Web hosting

A service offered to store and serve your web pages. Sometimes includes databases, scripting, and other internet services such as email.

Web safe

A limited set of fonts or colors that can be (virtually) guaranteed to display correctly on all computer systems.

Web server

A computer connected to the internet that serves up web pages (and often other network services such as email). Requires server software, such as Apache.

Web standards

A set of standards and specifications describing aspects of the web, as defined by the W3C.

Wireframes

"Storyboards for interactivity" is the best definition of wireframes I've heard yet! These are simplified, nondesigned diagrams detailing functional aspects of a website.

XHTML

Like HTML, but the X stands for "extensible." It is essentially a reformulation of regular HTML as XML.

Index

A

10-second rule 24
acceptance testing 23
accessibility 74-83
Actions menu 58-61
AdSense 106-7
advanced web design 92-122
Ajax 98-99
Alpha channel 48
Alt text 75, 84-85, 89, 97
alternative content 79
Analytics 93
animations
  embedded objects 93
  GIF files 47, 49
  plug-ins 92
  portfolios 118-19
  rollovers 99, 109-11
  rotating logo syndrome 25
  search engines 89
  web standards 79
Apache 112, 115
aqua-style buttons 48
aspect ratios 38
automated accessibility
  validation 79

B

back button 98
backgrounds 42, 100-101
backups 54-55
bandwidth 19, 62
batch processing 58-61
behaviors 108-9
bevel effects 94
bit depth 26, 31

blogging services 14, 19
body tags 45
bold text 50, 76
branding 68
break tags 76, 83
broadband 19
browsers 53, 56, 76
build phase 23
bullet points 41, 64, 70, 103
buttons 40, 41, 48, 119

C

caching 53
camel case 47
cascading style sheets
  (CSS) advanced 94, 98,
    100-105, 110-11
  Ajax 98
  basics 44, 46-47
  classes 46, 52-53, 68, 82
  columns 56-57
  drop shadows 42-43
  headers and footers 68-69
  ids 47, 52-54, 56-57,
    68-69, 94, 111
  menus 100-101
  rollovers 102-5, 110-11
  semantic markup 82-83
classes 46, 52-53, 68, 82
closing tags 46
code coloring 42
color theory 26, 32-33, 42-43
color-coding 33
columns 56-57, 102
comment tags 63
compatibility 76

complementary colors 26
compression 26, 28
contact links 66-67
content
  cascading style sheets 52
  changing/expanding 42
  copyright 17, 39, 115
  layout 56-57
  management systems 62
  search engines 87
  taxonomies 13
  see also images; text
contrast 75
control panels 114
copyright 17, 39, 115
counters 19
crawlers 84
credit lines 43
cropping images 43
CSS see cascading style
  sheets

D

databases 62
date displays 105
design basics 6, 23, 24-43
dictionary attacks 116
digital photography 26
directories 84, 112-13
divs
  columns 56-57
  comments 63
  drop shadows 35-37
  floated elements 47,
    56-57, 69
fonts 30-31

headers and footers
    68-69
  menus 94
  PHP includes 54
  rollovers 102, 111, 122
dotted lines 65
download time 19, 29
Dreamweaver 98
drop shadows 34-35, 42-43,
    48, 110
drop-down menus 76

E

eBay 55
email 66-67, 116
embedded objects 93, 115
emphasis tags 50, 82
exact phrase searches 86
expanding page design 35-37
exporting 58, 60, 97, 109
extensible markup
    language (XML) 98
external media 54-55
external style sheets 69

F

FAQ lists 62
feel/tone 25, 33
Fireworks 68, 108-9
fixed width design 36
Flash 79, 89, 92-93, 96-97,
    109-11, 118-19
floated elements 47, 56-57,
    69
fonts 30-31

footers 35, 65, 68-69, 101,
    104, 111
forums 18

G

galleries 8-11
GAWDS 78
GIF files 26, 29, 31, 47,
    48-49, 99
glow effects 110
Google 84, 86, 87, 93, 95,
    106-7
graphical text 84
Guild of Accessible Web
  Designers (GAWDS) 78

H

hacking 116-17
headers 35, 65, 68-69, 101, 111
headings 45, 50, 80-81, 88
hidden code 63
highlighting 94, 110
home pages 12-13, 14, 39
horizontal rollover menus
    110-11
hosting companies 62
house-building analogy 21
htaccess 112-13, 114, 117
hypertext markup language
  (HTML)
  advanced 94, 96, 98,
    100-101
  Ajax 98
  basics 43-45, 50-53
  code coloring 43
  Fireworks 68

Flash 96
headers and footers
    68-69
  links 66-67
  lists 64-65, 70-71
  menus 100-101
  portfolios 72-73
  search engines 87
  semantic markup 80-83
  source code 19, 63
  see also cascading
    style sheets

I

ids 47, 52-54, 56-57, 68-69,
    94, 111
image tags 51, 97
images
  Alt text 75, 89
  background 100-101
  batch processing 58-61
  borders 94, 118
  cropping 43
  Flash portfolios 118-19
  formats 38
  online portfolios 72
  PHP portfolios 120-22
  protection 115
  quality 28
  replacing 30
  size 28, 37, 58-59, 73
in-bound links 43, 86,
    88-89, 115
includes 54
inclusive web design 74-83

information architecture 13-15, 17
interactivity 6, 11
italic text 50, 82

J
JavaScript 98, 107
JPEG files 28, 32, 58-61, 72, 73, 101

K
keylines 30, 64-65
keywords 85, 90-91, 106

L
launch 23
links
credit lines 43
external style sheets 69
home page 14, 39
HTML tags 51, 66-67
in-bound 43, 86, 88-89, 115
permission 17
rollovers 41
liquid design 36
lists 21, 70-71, 102-3, 115
localization 86
logos 39

M
mailing lists 18
mailto links 66-67
manuals 44
maximum width 37, 41
menus 16, 21, 56-57, 76, 101-5, 108-11

meta tags 90-91
Microsoft Word 51, 52
misspellings 85, 87
movies 38
multiple domains 62
MySQL 116

N
naming divs/classes 68
navigation 13, 16, 29
nested lists 71
new windows 76, 94
Nielsen, Jakob 20
nonrepeating background patterns 42

O
obfuscation 117
object tags 97
off-topic posting 18
online portfolios 72-73
opacity 33, 42
opening tags 46
optimization 49, 59
optimum keyword density 91
ordered lists 21, 70-71

P
page looks 35
page-specific meta descriptions 91
palettes 32-33
paragraph tags 83
parameters 46
PAS 78-79
passwords 112-14, 116

PayPal 55
percentages 41
permission 17
photography 25, 26, 94, 118
Photoshop 58-61
PHP includes 54, 105, 120-22
planning 12-13, 22
plug-ins 92
PNG files 48-49
portfolios 72-73, 118-22
previewing 72
production techniques 44-73
project specification 22
proposals 22
prototyping 68
Publicly Available Specification (PAS 78) 79

R
relevant content 87
repeating background patterns 42
replacing images 30
resizeable text 78
resizing images 28
rollovers 41, 99, 100-105, 108-11, 122
rotating backup strategy 55
rotating logos 25
rounded corners 26, 40

S
sans-serif fonts 30-31
Save for Web 59
screen size 36-37, 40
scripting languages 62

search engine optimization (SEO) 84, 87, 88-90
search engines 84-91, 97
self-close tags 76, 83
semantic markup 80-83
SEO see search engine optimization
serif fonts 30
servers 56
shared hosting 62
shareware 19
site
build 23
maps 14-15, 77
searches 86, 95
sketches 32
software 19, 44, 51, 96-99
source code 19, 63
spamming 84, 85, 90, 116
spelling 85, 87
standards-compliant code 51, 74-83, 88, 96, 98
statistics 19, 93
storyboards 17, 22
strong text 76, 82
subheadings 81, 88
submenus 16
submit buttons 40, 41

T
tables 21, 34, 51, 83
target
audiences 16
image size 73
parameters 94
taxonomies 13

technical support 62
templates 23, 34
text
Alt text 75, 84-85, 89, 97
color theory 33, 75
fonts 30-31
graphical 84
highlighted 94
HTML tags 50, 76
resizeable 78
search engines 89
semantic markup 80-83
text editors 51
third-party scripts 116
three-column layouts 57
thumbnails 43, 120
tints 33, 42
tone/feel 25, 33
transparency 29, 48-49
two-column layouts 56

U
unordered lists 70
usability testing 20-21, 23, 56
usernames 112-14

V
validators 79
visitor numbers 19, 93
visual impairments 75, 78, 82

W
W3C 74-76, 79
watermarks 115

Web Content Accessibility Guidelines (WCAG) 79
web standards 51, 74-83, 88, 96, 98
web safe
colors 26, 31
fonts 31
wireframes 17, 22
Word 51, 52
World Wide Web Consortium (W3C) 74-76, 79
WYSIWWYG editors 50

X
XML see extensible markup language

Y
Yahoo! 84

Acknowledgments

The author would like to thank his colleagues at Message for their ideas and support, and all of the contributors who kindly lent their designs to this book. Thanks also to Neil Gibb for putting my name into the hat for this book, Chris Middleton for commissioning me, and my editor Jane Roe at RotoVision for showing me how to do it. Special thanks, as always, to Jo.